Crayola Dream~Makers®
Building fun and creativity into standards-based learning

Social Studies

K through 6

Ron De Long, M.Ed.
Janet B. McCracken, M.Ed.
Elizabeth Willett, M.Ed.

A Hallmark Company

© 2007 Crayola, LLC
Easton, PA 18044-0431

Acknowledgements

This guide and the entire Crayola® Dream-Makers® series would not be possible without the expertise and tireless efforts of Ron De Long, Jan McCracken, and Elizabeth Willett. Your passion for children, the arts, and creativity are inspiring. Thank you. Special thanks also to Julia Sefton for her content-area expertise, writing, research, and curriculum development of this guide.

Crayola also gratefully acknowledges the teachers and students who tested the lessons in this guide:

Barbi Bailey-Smith, Little River Elementary School, Durham, NC

Susan Bivona, Mount Prospect Elementary School, Basking Ridge, NJ

Billie Capps, Little River Elementary School, Durham, NC

Patricia Check, Freemansburg Elementary School, Freemansburg, PA
     and Governor Wolf Elementary School, Bethlehem, PA

Judi Collier, Little River Elementary School, Durham, NC

Trish Davlantes, Jordan Community School, Chicago, IL

Regina De Francisco, Mount Prospect Elementary School, Basking Ridge, NJ

Ron De Long, Weisenberg Elementary School, Kutztown, PA

Marcia Elise Effinger, Tipps Elementary School, Houston, TX

Pam Gall, Maple Avenue Middle School, Littlestown, PA

Barbara Kozero, Freemansburg Elementary School, Freemansburg, PA

Pam Leister, Jordan Community School, Chicago, IL

Abbie Lezak, Saucon Valley Middle School, Hellertown, PA

Elyse Martin, Jordan Community School, Chicago, IL

Judy Mazzucco, Millstone Township Elementary School, Clarksburg, NJ

Jen O'Flaherty, Sandy Plains Elementary School, Baltimore, MD

Jennifer Parks, T.J. Lee Elementary School, Irving, TX

Neila Steiner, C.S. 102, Bronx, NY

Elizabeth Willett, Applied Learning Center, Fort Worth, TX

Bobbi Yancey, College Oaks Elementary School, Lake Charles, LA

Sandy Young, Williamsport Elementary School, Williamsport, PA

Cathy Ziegenfuss, Paxinosa Elementary School, Easton, PA

Marilyn Zoller Koral, Everett Middle School, San Francisco, CA

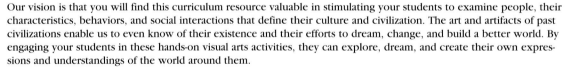

Our vision is that you will find this curriculum resource valuable in stimulating your students to examine people, their characteristics, behaviors, and social interactions that define their culture and civilization. The art and artifacts of past civilizations enable us to even know of their existence and their efforts to dream, change, and build a better world. By engaging your students in these hands-on visual arts activities, they can explore, dream, and create their own expressions and understandings of the world around them.

Nancy A. De Bellis
Director, Education Marketing
Crayola

Crayola Dream-Makers is a series of standards-based supplemental curriculum resources that contain lesson plans for educators teaching kindergarten through 6th grade. Each guide uses visual art lessons to stimulate critical thinking and problem-solving for individual subject areas such as Math, Language Arts, Science, and Social Studies. Students demonstrate and strengthen their knowledge while engaging in creative, fun, hands-on learning processes.

Printed in the United States of America
ISBN: 0-86696-324-4

Table of Contents

Crayola Dream-Makers: Catalyst for Creativity! 4

Lessons

A Forest of Family Trees 6   Family history
Stars of Fame 10   Roles & relationships
Design Diversity Figures 14   Culture & ethnicity
Map Your Space 18   Mapping
Business Card Business 22   Visual communication
Get Out the Vote! 26   Political processes
Let's Go Letterbox Hunting! 30   Orienteering
We Are the Children 34   Cultural traditions
Action Makes Dreams Come True 38   Social issues
Noticeable Norens 42   Business symbols
Interactive Timeline 46   Historical records
Protect an Invention 50   Model-making
Time to Cool Down Fans 54   Interpersonal communication
Things Are Not Always as They Appear 58   Imagination
Heroes and Heroines Wanted! 62   Responsibility
Compassion as Your Co-Pilot 66   Caring for others
Mindful Masks 70   Communicating emotions
"Reigning Respect" Crowns 74   Respectful behaviors
Scepters for Benevolent Leaders 78   Honoring authority
Gifts From the Heart 82   Teamwork
Honest to Goodness Fortunes 86   Trustworthiness
What's in a Name? Alternatives to Name-Calling! 90   Positive relationships
The "Try Again" Marionette 94   Perseverance
No Matter How You Look At It! 98   Uniqueness

Choosing Crayola Art Supplies 102

Each Crayola Dream-Makers guide provides elementary classroom and art teachers with 24 arts-focused lessons that extend children's learning and enhance academic skills. Align these lessons with your school district and state curriculum standards. Stay flexible in your teaching approaches with adaptations like these.

- **Be prepared.** Read through the lesson first. Create an art sample so you understand the process.
- **Discover new resources**. Each lesson contains background information, fine art and craft examples, representative student artwork, vocabulary builders, and discussion ideas. Use these suggestions as a springboard to find resources that address your students' interests and are pertinent to your community. Search Web sites such as Google Image to locate fine art. Stretch student imaginations and their awareness of the world around them.
- **Seek creative craft materials.** Ask children's families and local businesses to recycle clean, safe items for project use-and take better care of the environment, too. *Recycle, Reuse, Renew!*
- **Showcase student achievements.** Create banners to accompany curriculum project displays in your class, school, or community. Post the lesson's standards-based objectives with displays to demonstrate broad-based student learning. Demonstrate how children's accomplishments have personal meaning and promote life-long learning through portfolio documentation.
- **Make this book your own.** Jot down your own ideas as you plan and reflect on students' learning experiences. Combine art techniques and lesson content to fit goals for your students and classroom. Substitute other transformative craft materials. With students, make content webs of possibilities for extending learning opportunities.
- **Build connections.** Collaborate with your students, other teachers, administrators, artists in residence, and community groups to plan lessons that are unique. Work together to promote creative thinking!
- **Write DREAM statements.** As part of the assessment process, students are asked to reflect on their work in a dream journal. Before the lesson, Dream statements are expected to, capture children's prior knowledge about each topic. After each lesson, students state in writing how they will use what they have learned and dream about possibilities for future exploration..
- **Funding resources.** Crayola Dream-Makers lesson plans have been used in school programs funded by a variety of federal, state, local, and private grants. For more information about grants and grant writing visit The Foundation Center at www.fdncenter.org.

The lessons in this book are intended to address content benchmarks and grade-level expectations in social studies along with a heavy concentration of key art concepts. All lessons are teacher- and student-tested and follow a consistent format to support you in planning creative, fun learning opportunities for your students.

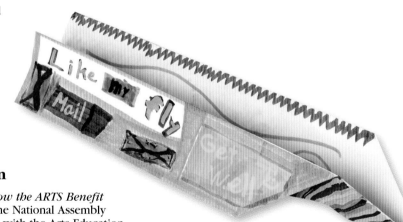

Benefits of Arts Integration

The 2006 report *Critical Evidence–How the ARTS Benefit Student Achievement*, published by the National Assembly of State Arts Agencies in collaboration with the Arts Education Partnership, identifies a number of ways that arts learning experiences benefit students. Teachers who consciously integrate arts-based practice into their teaching bring these benefits to their students.

> "Certain arts activities promote growth in positive social skills, including self-confidence, self-control, conflict resolution, collaboration, empathy, and social tolerance. Research evidence demonstrates these benefits apply to all students, not just the gifted and talented. The arts can play a key role in developing social competencies among educationally or economically disadvantaged youth who are at greatest risk of not successfully completing their education." (p. 14)

According to Diane Watanabe and Richard Sjolseth, co-directors of the Institute of Learning, Teaching, and the Human Brain, when there is joy in learning, student achievement soars.

> "When students find joy in their creative outlets, there is a positive carryover to school in general. Emotion, interest, and motivation promote learning and memory. Brain research shows the brain produces as least three pleasure chemicals when joy is present: endorphins, dopamine, and serotonin. These chemicals account for the emotional states produced by self-satisfaction, positive self-image, passion for one's art, and joy in learning." (2006, p. 20)

Children learn in many different ways

Howard Gardner has identified eight types of intelligences and may add others. Arts-integrated learning experiences enable children to more fully develop a wide range of skills and understandings.

- **Linguistic intelligence** involves sensitivity to spoken and written language, the ability to learn languages, and the capacity to use language to accomplish certain goals.
- **Logical-mathematical intelligence** consists of the capacity to analyze problems logically, carry out mathematical operations, and investigate issues scientifically.
- **Musical intelligence** involves skill in the performance, composition, and appreciation of musical patterns.
- **Bodily-kinesthetic intelligence** entails the potential of using one's whole body or parts of the body to solve problems.
- **Spatial intelligence** involves the potential to recognize and use the patterns of wide space and more confined areas.
- **Interpersonal intelligence** is concerned with the capacity to understand the intentions, motivations and desires of other people. It allows people to work effectively with others.
- **Intrapersonal intelligence** entails the capacity to understand oneself, to appreciate one's feelings, fears, and motivations.
- **Naturalist intelligence** enables human beings to recognize, categorize, and draw upon certain features of the environment. (Gardner, 1999: pp. 41-43, 52)

Find More Resources at www.crayola.com/educators

Supplementary materials for Dream-Makers guides include:

- Printable certificates for recognizing children's participation and adults' support
- Thousands of images of children's art
- Demonstration videos for teaching arts-integrated lessons
- Lesson-by-lesson correlations to California, New York, Texas, Illinois, and Florida standards
- Printable resource guides for educators and administrators
- More than 1,000 free, cross-curricular lesson plan ideas on wide-ranging topics, all developed by experienced educators. Sign up for free monthly newsletters to keep you abreast of the newest Crayola products, events, and projects.

Bibliography

Gardner, H. (1999). *Intelligence Reframed: Multiple Intelligences for the 21st Century.* New York: Basic Books.

Marzano, R.J. (March 2005). *ASCD Report–Preliminary Report on the 2004-05 Evaluation Study of the ASCD Program for Building Academic Vocabulary.* Reston, VA: Association for Supervision and Curriculum Development.

National Assembly of State Arts Agencies (NASAA) in collaboration with the Arts Education Partnership. (2006). *Critical Evidence–How the ARTS Benefit Student Achievement.* Washington, DC: Author.

Smith, M.K. (2002). Howard Gardner and multiple intelligences. The encyclopedia of informal education, http://www.infed.org/thinkers/gardner.htm. Retrieved from http://www.infed.org/thinkers/gardner.htm May 9, 2007. Reprinted with permission.

Watanabe, D., & Sjolseth, R. (2006). *Lifetime Payoffs: The Positive Effect of the Arts on Human Brain Development.* Miami, FL: NFAA youngARTS. Reprinted with permission.

A Forest of Family Trees

Objectives

Students identify the unique qualities of their families' histories and current interests and beliefs.

Students create images that represent their families' characteristics. These trees become part of a class forest in which children recognize similarities among their families.

Multiple Intelligences

Interpersonal
Intrapersonal
Naturalist
Spatial

What Does It Mean?

Extended family: people who have a close relationship to one another by birth, adoption, or other circumstances

Genealogy: the study of family history

Nuclear family: typically parents and their children

National Standards

Visual Arts Standard #2 Uses knowledge of structures and functions	**Social Studies Standard #4** Individual Development and Identity—experiences that provide for the study of individual development and identity.
	Health Education Standard #2 Students will analyze the influence of family, peers, culture, media, technology, and other factors on health behaviors.

Background Information

People in cultures around the world have always been interested in *who* and *where* they came from. Family history was originally passed from generation to generation orally. The term *genealogy*, comes from two Greek words meaning family and science. Recording *family* history has become a *science* that requires much research and record keeping.

Many people make decorative family trees. Family trees designs were often decorated with angels, wreaths, banners, and pictures of family members. Family Bibles often contained smaller versions of family trees. Many women made embroidered and quilted versions of family trees.

Resources

Climbing Your Family Tree: Online and Off-Line Genealogy for Kids by Ira Wolfman
Updated version of the author's excellent *Do People Grow on Family Trees?* Companion Web site is a useful tool for computer-savvy students from 5th to 8th grade.

Through the Eyes of Your Ancestors: A Step-by-Step Guide to Uncovering Your Family's History by Maureen Taylor
Loaded with inspiring historical photographs. Clear and helpful guide for upper-elementary and middle school students. Filled with practical forms and explanations of genealogical terms.

Who's Who in My Family? by Loreen Leddy
For 5- to 8-year-olds. A story of a classroom of animals sharing about their families. Illustrates the variety of different types of families and begins to explain how people are related within extended families.

Vocabulary List

Use this list to explore new vocabulary, create idea webs, or brainstorm related subjects.

Ancestor
Belief
Cousin
Culture
Custom
Descendant
Extended
Family
Father
Forbearer
Genealogical
Genealogy
Grandparent
Heritage
History
Lineage
Member
Mother
Nuclear
Offspring
Oral
Parent
Past
Recorded
Relation

Relative
Religion
Sibling
Single
Step
Study
Tradition
Written
Value

Artwork by students from
Saucon Valley Elementary School,
Hellertown, Pennsylvania.
Teacher: Mrs. Stephanie Laudenslager

Artwork by students from
St. Theresa School,
Hellertown, Pennsylvania.

Artwork by students from
Saucon Valley Elementary School,
Hellertown, Pennsylvania.
Teacher: Mrs. Stephanie Laudenslager

A Forest of Family Trees

	K-2	3-4	5-6
Suggested Preparation and Discussion	Display simple family trees in a variety of formats. Display sample of this art project to inspire children's creativity.		
	Read *Who's Who in My Family?* or similar book. Explain nuclear and extended families. Discuss children's families: shared interests, ideas, traditions, and beliefs. Create a list of ways families are alike/different. Look at trees. Describe the parts of a tree. What part unifies the tree? What tree parts extend outward? In what ways is an extended family like a tree?	Ask students to reflect on questions such as these. How is your family like your friends' families? How is it different? What holds your family together? What are the interests, traditions, beliefs, and values that your extended family shares? Consider geography, immigration and migration patterns, and other influences on family formation and traditions. Why are family histories often called family trees? Think about the parts of a tree and describe the purposes of each part. In what ways are the structures of trees and families similar?	Ask students to think about what defines a family. How has your family changed from when you were younger? What factors influence your family? What role does your family history play in your self-identity? Explore the influences of immigration, migration, jobs, social changes, economics, and other issues on changes in family structures and relationships. Will the concept of a family tree work structurally for your family? What if your tree is split? Or the branches tangled? Maybe an oak tree doesn't work but a bamboo patch does. Sketch the structure of your extended family. What shape does it have?
Crayola® Supplies	• Construction Paper™ Crayons • Markers • Model Magic® • School Glue • Scissors		
Other Materials	• Cardboard • Chenille stems • Construction paper • Hole punch • Recycled cardboard tubes		
Set-up/Tips	• Ask families to recycle cardboard tubes from gift wrap, plastic wrap, and paper towels. • Suggest that students work together to hold pieces in place for each other while assembling their trees.		

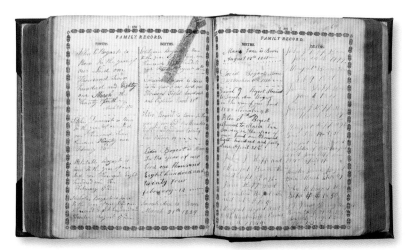

Bogart Family Bible History
Circa 1648
Printed paper
10 1/2" x 16"
Collection of Randy Granger.

Ruth Adams Family Tree
Circa, 1900
Artist unknown
Needlework on cotton
The Boyer/Adams Collection
Historic Bethlehem Partnerships, Inc.
Bethlehem, Pennsylvania

	K-2	3-4	5-6
Process: Session 1 20-30 min.	1. Cut and color enough leaves to have at least one for each family member. 2. Write names, interests, and/or family values on each one. Teacher assists emerging writers with labeling the symbol, photo, or words. 3. Decorate leaves with crayons and markers.		
Process: Session 2 20-30 min.	4. Decorate a cardboard tube to look like the tree trunk. 5. Cut a cardboard circle for the tree base. Make it at least three times as wide as the cardboard tube. Cut one end of cardboard tube into short, half-inch tabs. Glue tree-trunk tabs to cardboard base. Air-dry the glue.		
Process: Session 3 20-30 min.	6. Cover the glued tabs with Model Magic compound decorations. Create tiny leaves, twigs, squirrels, or other items that look natural at the bottom of a tree. 7. Punch two holes in each leaf. Thread chenille stem ends through them to make branches. 8. Bunch branches together. Hold them in place with another chenille stem. Place branches into top of tree trunk. Leave 2/3 of the branches outside the trunk. Bend stems to resemble branches. 9. Secure branches in the trunk with Model Magic compound.		
Assessment	• Observe whether children's family trees are unique. Do they include several family members, friends, and even pets?	• Students accurately describe unique features of their family trees to class.	• Students identify unique aspects of their family's history and how these characteristics help define who they are.
	• Students point out similarities between individuals on their family trees and people, traditions, or other characteristics represented by other family trees. • Ask students to reflect on this lesson and write a DREAM statement to summarize the most important things they learned.		
Extensions	Ask children to bring family photos to share with the class. Young children and those with special needs could complete this project with the assistance of family members.	Suggest that students list some questions they could use to find out more information about their families' genealogies. Create a list of people in family to interview. Introduce the topic of adoption. Invite an adult or older student who feels comfortable to talk about his/her adoption story. Encourage children to share how they see adoption. Resources to help create a positive learning experience on this theme are available from C.A.S.E., Center for Adoption Support and Education.	Write a journal entry from the perspective of another person's family history. Explore current family issues such as surrogate parents, nature vs. nurture, cloning, and the impact of these issues on future genealogical research. Ask gifted students to discuss Leo Tolstoy's quote "All happy families are the same, all unhappy families are unhappy in their own special way."

The Thankful Tree
2004
Artists: Margie Bell, Tina Butterfield, Donna Allison, Melissa Moser
Paper maché, paint, cardboard, glue, and construction paper
3' x 3' x 3'
Easton, Pennsylvania
Collection of Crayola LLC.

Stars of Fame

Objectives

Students identify their roles within groups including family, classroom, and friends in order to grasp how every individual is unique in various situations.

Students create representative stars that symbolize the roles they play in the lives of others.

Multiple Intelligences

Interpersonal   Linguistic

Intrapersonal

National Standards

Visual Arts Standard # 1 Understanding and applying media, techniques, and processes	**Social Studies Standard #5** Individuals, Groups, and Institutions—experiences that provide for the study of interactions among individuals, groups, and institutions.
	Health Education Standard #2 Students will analyze the influence of family, peers, culture, media, technology, and other factors on health behaviors.

Background Information

People like Mother Teresa are very fine examples of famous people who are stars because of the good things they do in their work and their lives. Our society recognizes people like this and considers them shining stars among all people.

In Hollywood, people in the motion pictures, television, radio, recording, or live theatre worlds are recognized on a famous sidewalk with a star. Each star includes the honoree's name and an emblem representing the area in which they worked.

Resources

Boy, You're Amazing by Virginia Kroll
Girl, You're Amazing by Virginia Kroll
Colorful, rhyming books of empowerment filled with quirky illustrations. Includes messages one is never too young to hear.

The Six Most Important Decisions You'll Ever Make:
A Guide for Teenagers by Sean Covey
Youth praise this book as a very helpful tool for preteens.

Unstoppable Me! Ten Ways to Soar Through Life
by Wayne Dyer
From the self-development guru, a book for ages 9 to 12. Encourages readers to strive for their dreams and provides catalyst for discussion.

Vocabulary List

Use this list to explore new vocabulary, create idea webs, or brainstorm related subjects.

Attribute
Balance
Characteristic
Contribution
Crayon resist
Dream
Empower
Esteem
Development
Growth
Highlight
Life
Personality
Quality
Rewarding
Role
Self
Shapes
Star
Symbols
Textures
Unique
Unity
Volunteer
Worth, self-worth

Artwork by students from
Millstone Township Elementary School,
Clarksburg, New Jersey
Teacher: Judy Mazzucco

What Does It Mean?

Crayon resist: art technique in which crayon is applied to parts of a surface and paint is applied on top so that the crayon wax resists the paint

Highlight: emphasis that draws attention to part of a work of art

Symbolize: use of an image to represent an idea or object

Crayola Dream~Makers®
Building fun and creativity into standards-based learning

Stars of Fame

	K-2	3-4	5-6
Suggested Preparation and Discussion	Read children's books that focus on students' roles as family member, student, friend, or club/team member. Choose titles that are relevant to children's lives, experiences, and cultures. Together, identify roles that children may typically have, such as brother/sister, friend, son/daughter, or volunteer. What symbols could represent these roles?	Discuss: Stars in the Hollywood Walk of Fame are decorated with one of five symbols. What roles do you hold in your life? What symbols might represent those roles? What colors, shapes, and textures help to convey your roles clearly to others? Do people's roles ever change? How and why? Can you play more than one role at a time? What roles do you find the most rewarding?	
Crayola® Supplies	• Crayons • Paint Brushes • School Glue • Scissors • Washable Paint		
		• Glitter Glue	
Other Materials	• Oak tag • Recycled newspaper • Water containers		
Set-up/Tips	• Cover painting area with newspaper.		

Artwork by students from
St. Theresa School,
Hellertown, Pennsylvania.

	K-2	3-4	5-6

Process: Session 1 20-30 min.	**Create, label, and decorate stars** 1. With crayons, students draw a large star on oaktag to represent themselves. 2. Draw at least five smaller stars, one for each role students play in their lives. Cut out stars.		
	3. Decorate stars with words and symbols using crayons.	3. Fill stars with words and symbols using crayons. Decorate the backs, too. Cut, fold, and glue additional same-size star shapes to the back of the large star to make it appear three-dimensional.	

Process: Session 2 15-20 min.	4. Paint the stars so each one looks unique. Notice the crayon-resist effects, and how the crayon colors "pop" out of the paint. Air-dry the paint.		

Process: Session 3 20-30 min.	**Assemble and apply star clusters** 5. Cut small strips of oak tag. Accordion-fold the strips. Glue folded strips to back of each small star. 6. Glue small stars to larger star to create a unified, balanced presentation. Air-dry the glue.		
		7. Highlight stars with Glitter Glue. Air-dry the glue.	

Assessment	• Is each personal star an accurate representation of the student? Did children make at least five unique stars that identify different roles? • Ask students to consider which stars best describe the students who created them. • Ask students to reflect on this lesson and write a DREAM statement to summarize the most important things they learned.		

Extensions	Choose someone to honor by naming a star in space. Identify leaders in the class, school, or community to honor with similar stars. Hold a presentation ceremony planned and carried out by the students. Form simple Model Magic® stars.	Watch the movie "It's a Wonderful Life." Ask students to imagine how their family's life would be different if one member were not part of the group. Write a skit or screenplay about a life event that focuses on the role of one person. Identify world leaders who have played major roles in other's lives. Design similar stars for them. Make folded stars like Tin Foil Twinkles on Crayola.com. Use them for ornaments or mobiles. Gifted students identify roles that they anticipate themselves as holding in the future. How will these roles complement and extend the person they are now? What roles may shift over time?	

Oakhurst Japanese Peace
Garden Recognition Award
Artist unknown
Engraved brass
3" x 3"
Private Collection.

Artwork by students from
St. Theresa School,
Hellertown, Pennsylvania.

Crayola **Dream~Makers®**
Building fun and creativity into standards-based learning

Objectives

Students compare characteristics found in dolls and sculptures of people in traditional clothing from different countries and cultures.

Students create figures using three-dimensional geometric shapes to accurately portray their own or another chosen cultural heritage.

Multiple Intelligences

Bodily-kinesthetic
Interpersonal
Intrapersonal

What Does It Mean?

Armature: a skeletal framework or support on which a sculpture is constructed in clay, wax, plaster, or other media

Three-dimensional shape: geometric forms such as spheres, cones, cylinders, cubes, pyramids, and rectangular prisms

National Standards

Visual Arts Standard #2 Understanding the visual arts in relation to history and culture	**Social Studies Standard #1** Culture—experiences that provide for the study of culture and cultural diversity.
	Health Education Standard #2 Students will analyze the influence of family, peers, culture, media, technology, and other factors on health behaviors.

Background Information

A very popular Russian craft is the creation of Matryoshka or nesting dolls. Inside a cylindrical, painted, wooden doll is another smaller doll, and inside that is another and so on until the last doll is so tiny that nothing fits inside of it.

These dolls were invented around 1890 in a workshop near Moscow. Craftspeople were dedicated to making crafts in an original Russian style, using traditional skills, designs, and ideas. Many of the designs painted on these dolls are based on folk and daily life images.

The name *Matryoshka* was a popular woman's name at the time. Its root is the Latin word for mother (mater).

Resources

Cornhusk, Silk, and Wishbones: A Book of Dolls From Around the World by Michelle Markell
Colorful alphabet book. Photographs of diverse and unique dolls from five continents. For children in grades 2 through 5.

Little Plum by Rumer Godden
For 9- to 12-year-olds. Old-fashioned storybook about Japanese dolls and their owners includes detailed line drawings.

The Magic Nesting Doll by Jacqueline K. Ogburn
A picture book as lush as a Russian lacquered box! Illustrations are painted like Matryoshka dolls. Perfect for kindergarten through grade 4.

Vocabulary List

Use this list to explore new vocabulary, create idea webs, or brainstorm related subjects.

Armature	Folk
Diversity	Form
Dolls	Global
Dress	Joining
Clothing	Matryoshka
Countries	Nesting
Craft	Russian
Culture	Sculpt
Figure/figurine	Toy
	Traditional/traditions
	Turned
	Wood
	World

Artwork by students from Jackson Elementary School, Williamsport, Pennsylvania.
Teacher: Sandy Young

Artwork by students from
St. Theresa School,
Hellertown, Pennsylvania.

Design Diversity Figures

	K-2	3-4	5-6
Suggested Preparation and Discussion	Display pictures and replicas of various types of dolls and similar figures reflective of a variety of world cultures. Ask families to display and discuss traditional figures whenever possible. Ask children to identify simple, three-dimensional shapes observed in the figures' forms such as spheres, cylinders, rectangles, and cubes that become the basis for more complex sculptural design. Discuss how designers include specific objects when they make figures to reflect a particular culture. Talk about clothing and accessories, and how they differ from culture to culture. Ask children to select one culture to portray with the figure they will sculpt—either a culture within their family or another with which they are familiar.		
Crayola® Supplies	• Markers • Model Magic® • Paint Brushes • School Glue • Watercolor Colored Pencils • Watercolor Paints		
Other Materials	• Modeling tools (such as toothpicks, craft sticks, and plastic dinnerware) • Paper bowls • Paper towels • Recycled newspaper • Water containers		
Set-up/Tips	• Ask students to bring in figures from around the world to exhibit. Toy catalogs and children's books are good visual resources for sculpted images. • Fresh Model Magic compound sticks to itself when pressed together. If pieces start to dry, join them with glue. • Sculpt larger-scale figures on armatures such as plastic water bottles or over recycled wire. • Cover painting surface with recycled newspaper. • Use water sparingly with watercolors to achieve the richest colors.		

Dine Navajo Dolls
2003
Artist: Alta Silago
Offcut fabric, beads, ribbon, cotton, threads, sequins
8 1/2" x 2 1/2" x 1 1/2"
New Mexico
Private Collection.

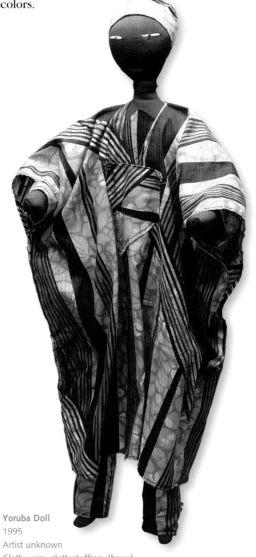

Yoruba Doll
1995
Artist unknown
Cloth, wire, cloth stuffing, thread
10" x 7" x 20"
South West Nigeria, Africa
Private Collection.

	K-2	3-4	5-6

Process:
Session 1
20-30 min.

Sculpt form

1. Shape a handful of Model Magic compound into a three-dimensional solid in the form of a human figure.

2. Model, pinch, and add texture to extend design using modeling tools.

3. Add arms, legs, head, hair, clothing, accessories, and additional distinctive features. Air-dry the sculpture for 24 hours.

Process:
Session 2
20-30 min.

Color figure

4. Dip watercolor pencils into water to soften. Draw features on dried figure.

5. Gently fill areas of the figure with watercolor washes. Air-dry the paint.

Process:
Session 3
20-30 min.

Glaze the sculpture

6. Add darker details, such as outlines and facial details, to figure with markers.

7. Mix equal amounts of school glue and water in a paper bowl. Brush on the figure. Air-dry the glaze.

Assessment

• Observe students during the creative process. Do students strive to accurately portray the human form? To represent authentic clothing and personal appearance?

• Invite students to exchange and study each other's dolls. What factors help them to identify the culture? Verify accuracy of representations.

• Ask students to reflect on this lesson and write a DREAM statement to summarize the most important things they learned.

Extensions

Insert a craft stick through bottom of newly sculpted figures to make puppets. Air-dry. Hold an around-the-world runway show where each child talks about what the figure is wearing and the country of origin.

With family members, prepare an international meal. Ask family members to attend in traditional clothing.

Younger students and some children with disabilities may find it helpful to work with a picture of the person and clothing they are sculpting.

Make similar, intricate sculptures using Crayola Air-Dry Clay and paint.

Research: Does the whole world wear jeans? Seek out cultures where people still wear their traditional clothing every day, not just for special events. Debate the impact of modernity on culture.

Suggest that gifted children research changes in a clothing accessory such as hats, shoes, or underclothes over time. In what ways have these items changed? Stayed the same? What changes are due to technology? To fashion?

Find out how traditional fabrics are made. Create authentic replicas. Consider lessons plans on Crayola.com such as African Asimevo Cloth, Suzani From Bukhara, Samoan Siapo Bark Cloth, and Scotland's Perfect Plaids.

Matryoshka Dolls
Above Left, Fairytale Matryoshkas
2004
Artist unknown
Turned wood, paint, gold leaf
6 1/2" x 3 1/4" x 3 1/4"
St. Petersburg, Russia
Private Collection.

Above Right, Kandinsky-like Matryoshka Dolls
2004
Artist unknown
Turned wood, paint
7 1/2" x 4" x 4"
St. Petersburg, Russia
Private Collection.

Crayola Dream~Makers®
Building fun and creativity into standards-based learning

Map Your Space

Objectives

Students observe and identify the features of a selected environment from an overhead perspective.

Students graphically organize and represent their ideas from the space on a map. Older students use graph paper to draw to scale.

Multiple Intelligences

Logical-mathematical
Naturalist
Spatial

National Standards	
Visual Arts Standard #3 Choosing and evaluating a range of subject matter, symbols and ideas	**Social Studies Standard #3** People, Places, and Environments—experiences that provide for the study of people, place, and environments.
	Health Education Standard #1 Students will comprehend concepts related to health promotion and disease prevention to enhance health.

Background Information

The first known map was made in the Middle East, on a clay tablet small enough to fit in your hand. It was drawn between 2300 and 2500 BCE! That's more than 4000 years ago. Experts think maps were probably used before then, although they haven't found any earlier examples. Computerized geographic information systems were developed in the 1960s, linking database information with maps to increase the amount of information that maps display.

Architects use maps called blueprints when they build homes. Often these maps or blueprint plans will show where all the features are placed in a room such as doors, windows, closets, and electrical outlets.

Interior designers also create maps of layouts of rooms in homes so they know where beds, dressers, chairs, and other furnishings will go.

Resources

As the Crow Flies: A First Book of Maps by Gail Hartman
Innovative book about maps for 5- to 8-year-olds. Explores the world from various animals' points of view.

Mapping Penny's World by Loreen Leedy
For second to fourth graders. Readable story follows a child's mapping of her room.

The Geography Book: Activities for Exploring, Mapping, and Enjoying Your World by Caroline Arnold
Hands-on learning experiences for third through sixth grades.

Vocabulary List

Use this list to explore new vocabulary, create idea webs, or brainstorm related subjects.

Atlas
Bird's-eye view
Blueprint
Cartography
Chart
Database
Dimension
Direction
Estimation
Graph
Key
Line
Map
Mapping
Maps
Models

Overhead view
Perspective
Place
Proportions
Region
Scale
Scale drawing
Shapes
Size
Space
Symbols
Visualize

Interior of a Farm House
1936
Artist: Thomas Hart Benton, American, 1889-1975
Tempera on board
18" x 30", SN950
Museum Purchase, Collection of The John and Mable Ringling Museum of Art, State Art Museum of Florida.

Artwork by students from
Brenham Elementary School,
Brenham, Texas.
Teacher: Marcia Elise Effinger

What Does It Mean?

Bird's eye view: a view from above, as if one were flying over the object

Cartography: the art of creating maps

Scale: accurate proportions when drawing two or more objects

Artwork by students from
St. Theresa School,
Hellertown, Pennsylvania.

Crayola **Dream~Makers**®
Building fun and creativity into standards-based learning

Map Your Space

	K-2	3-4	5-6
Suggested Preparation and Discussion	Tour a construction site or building for which blueprints can be studied. Match details on the plans with the actual construction. Point out which blueprints represent a bird's-eye (overhead) view. Take a concrete, visual tour of the classroom. Ask students to find forms, shapes, architectural details (doors, windows), and other features. Point out where items are located in relationship to one another. Help children visualize the classroom from directly overhead by making block structures, models with cardboard boxes, or other 3-D representations that can be viewed from above.	Display various types of maps of your state—road maps, geologic surveys, relief, elevation. Study map keys to determine what symbols and colors represent. Locate your community on each map. Mark major cities, landmarks, industries, rivers, historic locations, and other important places.	Examine local, regional, and global maps, including artistic renderings and historical maps. Explore concepts such as scale, estimation, dimensions, direction, and mapping symbols. Note that the dimension of the drawing is always listed first: 1 inch = 40 miles Demonstrate and have students practice using graph paper to draw to scale. Start with a small, observable item such as an apple, to enlarge. Then experiment with reducing the size of a familiar item, such as a car. Ask children to choose a region of interest to them to map to scale.
Crayola® Supplies	• Colored Pencils • Gel Markers • Paint Brushes • Scissors • Tempera Paint		
Other Materials			• Ruler • Graph paper
	• Craft paper • Oak tag • Recycled newspaper • Ribbon • Water containers • White paper		
Set-up/Tips	• Cover painting surface with newspaper. • Apply paint sparingly to keep paper from curling. • Use an overhead projector or computer to demonstrate the process of enlarging or reducing to scale.		

Artwork by students from
St. Theresa School,
Hellertown, Pennsylvania.

	K-2	3-4	5-6
Process: Session 1 20-30 min.	**Decorate map back** 1. Cut craft paper into a size suitable for the map. 2. Decorate one side. Use designs such as lines, dots, shapes, and symbols common in blueprints or cartography. Air-dry the paint.		
Process: Session 2 15-20 min.	**Sketch map** 3. On plain paper, sketch the classroom or your bedroom shape—from a bird's-eye view—to fill the map space. Include all walls. 4. Locate doors and windows. Mark placement of furniture.	**Sketch map** 3. On plain paper, sketch the borders of the state. Make it large enough to fill the map space. 4. Mark positions of geographic landmarks such as mountains, bodies of water, and cities.	**Sketch map** 3. Choose the scale for the map, making sure the map will fit on the craft paper. Sketch selected region on graph paper. 4. Mark positions of geographic landmarks such as mountains, bodies of water, state/province or national borders, and cities.
Process: Session 3 20-30 min.	**Draw map** 5. Using map draft as a guide, copy map on plain side of craft paper with Gel Markers. Use common symbols to indicate details. 6. Label important features. 7. Prepare a key to map symbols. 8. Roll map into cylinder. Tie ribbon around it.		**Draw map** 5. With a ruler, mark a light grid on the plain side of the craft paper. 6. Translate region from smaller graph paper to larger map with Gel Markers. 7. Label important features. 8. Develop a key to map symbols including the scale.
Assessment	• Do maps accurately represent the classroom from an overhead perspective? Are all major features included?	• Do maps accurately represent the state? • Are major landmarks included and labeled properly?	• How precise is the scale drawing of the region? Is the graph paper draft accurately enlarged on the final map? Is the scale indicated with the drawing measurement first?
	• Is back of map designed in an aesthetically pleasing way? • Are map symbols and key easy to understand and accurate? • Ask students to reflect on this lesson and write a DREAM statement to summarize the most important things they learned.		
Extensions	Display maps of the school, neighborhood, city, and state. Locate the school and students' homes. Study examples of different types of graphic representations of space such as weather maps, relief maps, and building models. Draw series of ever-expanding views of the classroom—start with a small detail such as a desk and move out from it to encompass big picture. Students with some types of disabilities may need to draw their maps with assistive technology.	Encourage students to share maps from places they have visited including museums, road, mass transit, topical, and imaginary maps. Identify locations with sticky dots. Explore contour maps. Create a 3-D contour map (to scale for older and gifted students). Discuss how and why maps distort distance, area, and shape. Compare the Peter's Projection with the Mercator Projection.	

Painted Map Design
Artist unknown
Painted wood
Collection of Nancy A. De Bellis.

Crayola **Dream~Makers®**
Building fun and creativity into standards-based learning

Objectives

Students identify professions or jobs that involve the production/manufacturing, distribution, or exchange of natural resources, goods, and/or services.

Students create personalized business cards with eye-catching logos to communicate across cultures and that represent a position within a chosen business in the economic system.

Multiple Intelligences

Linguistic
Logical-mathematical

What Does It Mean?

Eye catching: graphic technique to get attention

Symbol: image that represents an idea or object

National Standards	
Visual Arts Standard #5 Reflecting upon and assessing the characteristics and merits of their work and the work of others	**Social Studies Standard #7** Production, Distribution, and Consumption—experiences that provide for the study of how people organize for the production, distribution, and consumption of goods and services. **Social Studies Standard #9 (Grades 5-6)** Global Connections—experiences that provide for the study of global connections and interdependence.
	Health Education Standard #4 Students will demonstrate the ability to use interpersonal communication skills to enhance health and avoid or reduce health risks.

Background Information

Early business cards were often called calling cards. The card only contained the name of an individual. When a person would call on a residence or business, the visitor would present or provide a calling card to identify themselves.

People who work in business today typically exchange business cards as a way of identifying themselves, who they work for and what they do to each other. Business cards typically contain the name of the business, the employee who works at the business, and the address and contact information that helps people connect to each other. Often the artwork, signs and symbols on the business card will provide clues about what the business manufacturers. Crayola business cards, for example, show a very colorful oval with a symbol that reflects a smile. This symbol was designed to let people know that Crayola products bring smiles to many people.

Resources

A Basket of Bangles: How a Business Begins
by Ginger Howard
Fictional account of a small business's history in Bangladesh. Starts with finding seed money and follows the process with text and illustrations. Aimed at grades 1 through 4. Some concepts may need further explanation.

The Kid's Guide to Business by Jeff Brown
Step-by-step instruction, for grades 4 through 8, about developing a business using a case-study format.

Work by Ann Morris
Photo essay about work around the world by the popular children's non-fiction author. Good stimulus for discussion with kindergarten and early elementary students.

Vocabulary List

Use this list to explore new vocabulary, create idea webs, or brainstorm related subjects.

Advertising	Interrelated industries
Branding	Job
Business	Letterhead
Capitalism	Logo
Card	Manufacturing
Company	Natural resources
Consumer	Online
Consumption	Organization
Distribution	Production
Economics	Start-up
Economy	Symbol
Emphasis	Title
Entrepreneur	Trade
Graphic	Transportation
Industry	Work
Interdependence	

Artwork by students from
Sandy Plains Elementary School,
Baltimore, Maryland.
Teacher: Jen O'Flaherty

Edwin Binney
Founder

Crayola
1100 Church Lane, PO Box 431
Easton, PA 18044-0431
T (610) 555-0100
F (610) 555-0199
E emailaddress.com
www.crayola.com

Crayola Business Card
Artist unknown

Crayola **Dream~Makers**
Building fun and creativity into standards-based learning

	K-2	3-4	5-6
Suggested Preparation and Discussion	Display business cards, especially those from families of children in the group. Show cards that display unique business names, attention-getting logos, employee names, and job titles that link directly to business.		
	Discuss jobs that children's parents, grandparents, and friends have. What is the work of students? Ask students to review magazines. Cut out business logos that catch their eye. Discuss why the logos gained attention.	Display books, tools, and products related to work, global economics, and business. Encourage students to discuss the importance of selecting a business name, identifying jobs to be done, and making an organization chart to support a business. Ask students to bring in examples of business cards. Discuss which ones work better than others and why.	
			Research the roles of natural resources, transportation, manufacturing, and distribution in the capitalism. How are they different in other economic systems?
Crayola® Supplies	• Colored Pencils • Markers • Paint Brushes • Scissors • Watercolor colored pencils		
Other Materials	• Oak tag • Recycled magazines Recycled newspapers • Water containers • White paper		
Set-up/Tips	• Cover watercolor area with newspaper. • Soften watercolor colored pencil tips by dipping or soaking them in water.		

Artwork by students from
St. Theresa School,
Hellertown, Pennsylvania.

	K-2	3-4	5-6

Process:
Session 1
20-30 min.

Form business teams and plans

1. Choose teams with four or five students. Teams cooperate to identify an imaginary business that supports and promotes their class or family (grades K-2), community/state (grades 3-4), or national business (grades 5-6).

2. Teams select business names and identify jobs and work titles.

Process:
Session 2
20-30 min.

Brainstorm business branding

3. Collaborate to sketch three potential designs for business cards. Cards include business name, student's name and job title, and eye-catching graphic or logo. Develop themes or slogans to describe the nature of the business.

4. Choose one logo and the colors to represent the business.

Process:
Session 3
20-30 min.

Create cards

5. Cut oak tag into business cards. Enhance the original sketch to maximize the impact of the chosen card. Make sure there is one point of emphasis!

6. Embellish the design using watercolor pencils. Create one card for each student, each with a different role in the business.

7. Enrich the design's impact by using a damp brush to fill the card with watercolor. Air-dry the cards.

8. Add details such as outlines and words with a dry colored pencil or markers.

Assessment

• Analyze and rank the business cards for their visual impact, communication strengths, understanding of business models, and artistic merit.

• Ask students to reflect on this lesson and write a DREAM statement to summarize the most important things they learned.

Extensions

Plan a business card exchange. Students design cards to represent themselves. Explain designs and business models to classmates.

Interview local small-business owners to find out how they got started. How did they design their logos? What resources were needed to start? How many people were involved? What were their jobs?

Children with special needs could design their cards with assistive technology.

Evaluate famous logos, brand names, and products. Consider other symbols or names that would be appropriate. Propose different logos and debate their efficacy.

Meanings of logos/symbols change. What was the original thinking behind the golden arches? (large size, symbol of welcome) Compare these to their meaning now.

Challenge gifted students to think about issues such as this one: "Made in Japan" used to be a derogatory term in the United States. Now Japanese cars are best sellers. Why did the situation change?

Visit a local small business. Talk with the owner about the challenges and rewards of owning a business.

What popular games deal with economics, such as Monopoly® (real estate) or the card game Pit® (stock market)? Ask students to invent a game with their business cards. What else do they need? A game board? Tokens? Spinner? Currency?

Artwork by students from
St. Theresa School,
Hellertown, Pennsylvania.

Crayola **Dream~Makers®**
Building fun and creativity into standards-based learning

Get Out the Vote!

Objectives

Students explore the political process in the United States and encourage each other to become more engaged in a classroom election.

Students create campaign posters, banners, signs, and/or buttons to help convince their classmates to support their candidacy for class office or an issue upon which the class will vote.

Multiple Intelligences

Interpersonal

Intrapersonal

What Does It Mean?

Balance: both sides of a design have the same visual weight

Emphasis: stress or importance

Proportion: relative size between two or more objects

National Standards

Visual Arts Standard #5 Reflecting upon and assessing the characteristics and merits of their work and the work of others	**Social Studies Standard #6** Power, Authority, and Governance—experiences that provide for the study of how people create and change structures of power, authority, and governance.
	Health Education Standard #8 Students will demonstrate the ability to advocate for personal, family, and community health.

Background Information

Political posters and buttons are part of election campaigns in the United States. Posters and buttons help voters know and understand for whom and for what they are voting. Old posters and buttons from presidential campaigns are often valued and considered collectible by people. Cornell University Libraries house the Susan H. Douglas Collection of Political Americana in their Division of Rare and Manuscript Collections. The collection consists of approximately 5,500 pieces of political memorabilia dating from 1789 to 1960 in the following categories: ballots, bric-a-brac (larger, three-dimensional objects), broadsides (small posters), buttons, cartoons, maps and charts, pamphlets, parade items, posters, prints, ribbons, sheet music, songbooks, textiles, trinkets, and wearing apparel. All were used for presidential elections, and the artifacts reflect the culture and people of the time.

Resources

Campaign Politics: What's Fair? What's Foul?
by Kathiann Kawalski
Contemporary analysis of the political scene in the United States. For middle-school students. Includes media roles in campaigns as well as election reform movements.

Class Election for the Black Lagoon by Mike Thayer
Young students will be able to clearly tell the "right and wrongs" of school campaigning. A humorous look at school elections.

Class President by Johanna Hurwitz
Hurwitz explores school elections involving children in the upper elementary grades.

So You Want to Be President? by Weston Woods
Another humorous look at presidents. Filled with anecdotes and trivia illustrating the variety of men who have held this office. For age 8 and older.

Vocabulary List

Use this list to explore new vocabulary, create idea webs, or brainstorm related subjects.

Ballot	Politics
Button	Poster
Campaign	Process
Candidate	Proportion
Cast	Promise
Election	Reform
Electoral	Run
Emphasis	Scale
Govern	Slogan
Government	Symbols
Leader	Unity
Media	Vote
Memorabilia	
Office	
Pattern	
Political	

Theodore Roosevelt
Campaign Poster
1904
Artist unknown
Colored print reproduction
18" x 24"
Pennsylvania
Collection of
Jim Matthews.

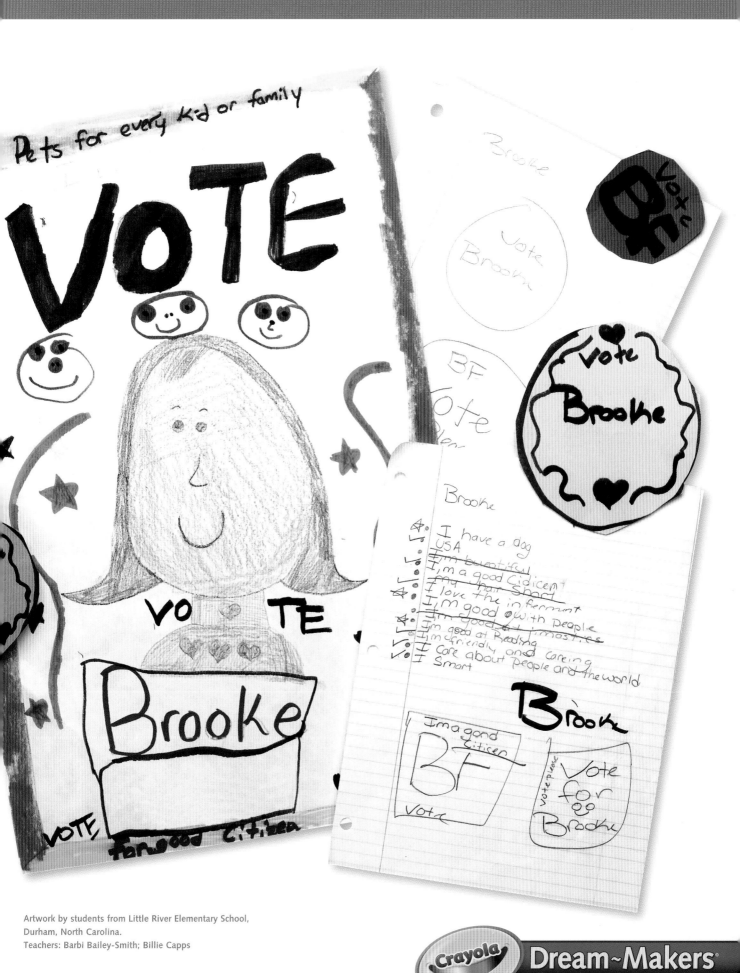

Artwork by students from Little River Elementary School,
Durham, North Carolina.
Teachers: Barbi Bailey-Smith; Billie Capps

	K-2	3-4	5-6
Suggested Preparation and Discussion	Find out what children know about voting and the electoral process. Focus on local issues and candidates. Who has gone along with someone when they voted? Discuss how someone becomes elected to an office—how votes are cast and counted plus who gets to vote. Talk about how candidates campaign to convince voters that they are the most-qualified person for the position and that the issues they support deserve attention.	Follow the election process during a campaign season. How do candidates call attention to their qualifications? Their issues? How does the campaign change as the election draws near? Discuss Thomas Jefferson's belief that people in the United States should campaign for the "Office of Citizen" to support the government and the common good. Everyone is responsible for respecting diversity, volunteering, joining community organizations, voting, and serving on juries.	

Display political photographs, posters, pamphlets, buttons, and other campaign materials collected from local, state, and national campaigns. How do these artifacts catch attention and help people make personal voting decisions? Discuss the importance of color, catchy slogans, and other visual effects in helping to capture votes.

Ask a candidate for office—from student council to school boards or other offices—to speak with the group about the importance of public service. How does it enrich the life of the candidate? Of the constituents?

Students list the qualities that they will bring to an elected office (K-2), the merits of their position on an issue (3-4), or the reasons why it is so important to vote (5-6).

Crayola® Supplies	• Colored Pencils • Glue Sticks • Markers • Scissors
Other Materials	• Masking tape • Poster board, oak tag, or card stock • Recycled file folders • White paper

Artwork by students from St. Theresa School, Hellertown, Pennsylvania.

Process: Session 1 20-30 min.

Create a poster

1. Consider ways to portray the points to be made in a visual way. Sketch poster ideas—words and symbols. Remember a poster has center, top, bottom, and border areas to visually energize. Consider emphasis, balance, and proportion in the design.

2. Scale up the drawing on larger, sturdier paper. Draw attention to the poster and create unity by filling shapes and spaces with colors or patterns.

Process: Session 2 20-30 min.

Design a campaign button

3. Choose the slogan and/or logo to include on the button.

4. Cut circles from recycled file folders. Design buttons on the circles or glue colorful paper to them first. Air-dry the glue.

5. Emphasize the slogan with dark lines or other effects. Fill the button with color for added punch.

6. Attach buttons on clothing with masking tape loops.

7. Display posters and buttons before a relevant election.

Assessment

- Conduct a classroom election. Measure the effectiveness of campaign materials by asking students to cast ballots based on visual appeal.

- Ask students to reflect on this lesson and write a DREAM statement to summarize the most important things they learned.

Extensions

Visit a local government building. Tour voter registration areas. See voting machines and learn how they operate.

Regularly vote on choices within the classroom such as which games to play at recess, how to thank a volunteer, or which book or poem to read aloud.

Computer-assisted drawing programs may be helpful for some children who have small-motor challenges.

Suggest that children work in small groups to brainstorm slogans, convincing get-out-the-vote strategies, and logo ideas.

Discuss: Is it always the best person for the office who wins the election? How can a country ensure that elections are fair? Learn more about election reform efforts.

Enjoy the movie "Napoleon Dynamite." Follow Pedro's infamous campaign for school president with its cultural errors and funny upsets. Write skits with similar incidents.

Gifted students could develop campaign materials to advocate for an issue such as care for the environment, year-round schools, or health care.

Collect position statements from various candidates. Hold a mock debate with different students taking the roles of the candidates.

Richard Nixon Campaign Buttons
1974
Artist unknown
Tin and paint
1" diameter
Pennsylvania
Collection of Ann Lesher.

Crayola **Dream~Makers**
Building fun and creativity into standards-based learning

Let's Go Letterbox Hunting!

Objectives

Students explore and implement the reverse-imagery printing/stamping process by creating printed papers and personal symbolic stamps.

Students design letterboxes, passbooks, logbooks, and detailed maps with visual and text clues that they use to lead the way to each other's hidden letterboxes.

Multiple Intelligences

Bodily-kinesthetic   **Logical-mathematical**

National Standards

Visual Arts Standard #2 Using knowledge of structures and functions	**Social Studies Standard #3** People, Places, and Environments—experiences that provide for the study of people, place, and environments.
	Health Education Standard #3 Students will demonstrate the ability to access valid information and products and services to enhance health.

Background Information

Letterboxing originated in England and is a hobby that is catching on in the United States. It combines orienteering (using a map and compass to navigate between check-points), rubber stamp collecting, and creativity in a unique activity that all ages can enjoy. The object of letterboxing is to collect stamp impressions from stamps hidden in various locations. These locations are found on letterboxing Web sites and include detailed maps and tricky clues. Finding the box is a challenge and makes collecting the stamps even more exciting. Letterbox participants often gather to share their adventures and stamps. Geocaching is a more technological version of letterboxing using a GPS.

Resources

The Letter Jesters by Cathryn Falwell
Colorful book introduces children, ages 5 through 8, to typography and typefaces.

The Letterboxer's Companion by Randy Hall
Handbook covers the basics of this puzzle-solving hobby for all ages.

The Usborne Book of Treasure Hunting by Anna Claybourne
Introduction to all types of treasure hunting. Contains full-color photographs and historical reproductions. For grades 4 through 6.

Vocabulary List

Use this list to explore new vocabulary, create idea webs, or brainstorm related subjects.

Chest
Challenge
Clue
Compass
Fortune
Geocaching
Hobby
Hunt
Hunting
Letter
Letterbox
Letterboxing
Logbook
Map
Navigate
Orienteering

Passbook
Print
Quest
Questing
Reverse imagery
Scavenger
Solve
Stamp/stamping
Symbols
Treasure
Trove

Artwork by students from
Saucon Valley Middle School,
Hellertown, Pennsylvania.
Teacher: Jenna Makos

Artwork by students from
St. Theresa School,
Hellertown, Pennsylvania.

= Library = Bunglow Mystery by
Nancy Drew
= Cafeteria = Plastic fork
Second Grade = Big pencil
Eighth Grade = Calculator
Playground = Small ball

Artwork by students from
Saucon Valley Middle School,
Hellertown, Pennsylvania.
Teacher: Jenna Makos

What Does It Mean?

Cache: hiding place for treasures

Geocaching: outdoor treasure hunt using global positioning systems (GPS)

Letterbox hunting: a treasure hunt in which players use clues to find boxes hidden in public places

Reverse imagery: when printed or stamped, the design appears backward from the original

Clues for finding Sarahs Box

	K-2	3-4	5-6
Suggested Preparation and Discussion	Engage in a simple scavenger hunts if children are unfamiliar with the concept or to improve their map-reading skills. Research the letterbox practice of collecting stamps in passbook as well as leaving personal stamp at letterbox logbook. If someone in the community has this pastime, invite them to explain it to the class. Display assorted maps, atlases, and books about treasure hunting and letterbox searches. Discuss the reasons for maps, the elements of maps, and their visual clues. Review the use of symbols in map keys.		
Crayola® Supplies	• Crayons • Glue Sticks • Model Magic® • Paint Brushes • Tempera Paint		
Other Materials	• Clean combs • Modeling tools such as craft sticks and plastic dinnerware • Oak tag • Recycled cardboard boxes with lids Recycled newspaper • Ribbon • Sponges • Water containers • White paper		
Set-up/Tips	• Ask families to donate small boxes with lids. • Cover painting surface with newspaper. • Close adult supervision is essential whenever children leave the classroom.		

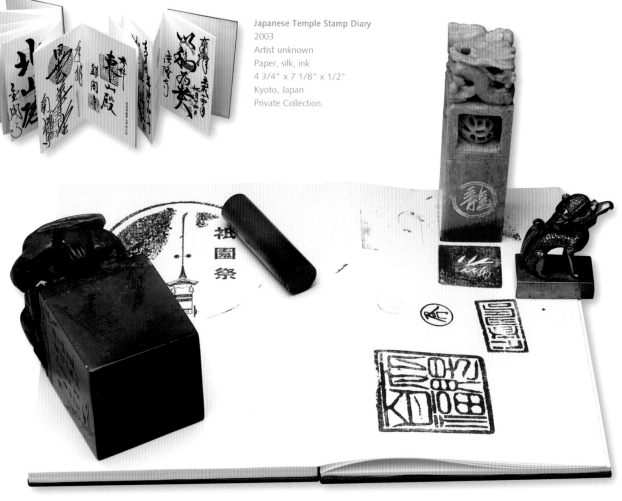

Japanese Temple Stamp Diary
2003
Artist unknown
Paper, silk, ink
4 3/4" x 7 1/8" x 1/2"
Kyoto, Japan
Private Collection.

Chops
Private Collection.
Left to right:

Chinese Zodiac Rabbit Chop	**Xu Bing Square Word Calligraphy Chop**	**Chinese Zodiac Dragon Chop**	**Griffin Chop**
Carved soapstone	Carved jade	Carved soapstone	Cast bronze
2" x 2" x 4"	2 1/4" x 1/2"	1 1/4" x 1 1/4" x 4"	1 3/8" x 3/8" x 2"

	K-2	3-4	5-6

**Process:
Session 1
20-30 min.**

Create monoprints

1. Spread a thin layer of paint evenly over oak tag or recycled file folders. Blend colors gently using brushes. Etch designs into paint with plastic combs or other tools.

2. Press white paper over etched design. Remove quickly. Repeat process to create enough prints to decorate passbook, logbook, and letterbox covers. Air-dry the prints.

**Process:
Session 2
20-30 min.**

Decorate letterboxes, logbooks, and passbooks

3. Cut printed paper to fit over boxes. Glue in place.

4. Fold another printed sheet in half for a passbook cover. Insert three or four sheets of folded, plain paper inside. Tie ribbon around centerfold to hold pages inside cover.

5. Repeat Step 4 to make logbooks to fit inside the letterboxes. Cut paper to size as needed.

**Process:
Session 3
10-15 min.**

Design stamps

6. Students shape a handful of Model Magic compound into thick letters with their first initials or other symbols. Press against flat surface to make smooth stamping bottom. Air-dry for 24 hours.

Design stamps

6. Form a handful of Model Magic compound into a stamp handle. Flatten the stamp face on a smooth surface. Roll thin "snakes" of modeling material. Use these to create a raised design on stamp bottom. Or incise a personal design into stamp face with modeling tools. Air-dry for 24 hours.

**Process:
Session 4
20-30 min.**

Prepare maps

7. In small groups or individually, pick places to hide letterboxes. Young children choose a spot within the classroom. Older children might decide to hide their boxes in the school and even on the school grounds.

8. With crayons, draw maps containing detailed visual clues to locate the boxes. Write additional text clues on the back of the map.

**Process:
Session 5
15-20 min.**

Hold the letterbox hunt

9. Students place logbooks and stamps in their letterboxes. They hide their letterboxes without being observed.

10. Children exchange maps and follow the clues to find each other's letterboxes.

11. To make a stamp pad, brush small amounts of paint over a clean, moist sponge. To print, students press the stamp found in letterbox into their passbooks.

12. After all letterboxes have been found, students press their own stamps into the logbook inside the letterbox they found.

Assessment

- Did children follow directions to make the printed papers? To cover their letterboxes and construct their logbooks and passbooks? To make their stamps? Did they successfully employ the reverse-image technique?

- Were maps sufficiently detailed and accurate that others could follow them to find letterboxes? Were both symbols and words used for clues?

- Ask students to reflect on this lesson and write a DREAM statement to summarize the most important things they learned.

Extensions

Younger students and those with some disabilities may be more successful in working with more skilled partners, especially during mapmaking.

Invite a Geocaching enthusiast to share adventures with class. Plan a Questing adventure.

Suggest that gifted students write an imaginary journal about letterbox hunting adventures. Where would they hide imaginary boxes? How would they find others?

Interview people who have gone letterbox hunting. How did they decide where to place their letterbox? What locations were their most difficult challenges to find?

To seal the dried stamps or prints, mix equal parts of Crayola School Glue and water. Brush or spray to coat the surface. Air-dry. Clean spray bottle thoroughly after use.

Crayola Dream~Makers®
Building fun and creativity into standards-based learning

We Are the Children

Objectives

Students observe detailed features in the historical and contemporary dress worn by peoples in diverse cultures, including those reflected in the collage art of Romare Bearden.

Students create paper figures of people dressed in clothing authentic for a specific time and culture, reflecting their knowledge and understanding of diversity.

Multiple Intelligences

Interpersonal	Spatial

National Standards	
Visual Arts Standard #4 Understanding the visual arts in relation to arts and cultures	**Social Studies Standard #9** Global Connections—experiences that provide for the study of global connections and interdependence
	Health Education Standard #2 Students will analyze the influence of family, peers, culture, media, technology and other factors on health behaviors.

Background Information

Collage art is a two-dimensional work of art containing pieces of paper, cloth, or other materials which are arranged and then glued to a flat surface. Many artists like Picasso created collage art where he cut out and glued newspaper and magazine shapes and glued them to his paintings. American artist like Romare Bearden (1911-1988) used collage to create images that reflected the African American heritage. He embedded his very complex collages with symbols that added meaning to his work and the story being told through it. Romare Bearden wanted people to think about his collage artworks. He hoped his collages would influence positive social behavior in people.

Resources

All the Colors of the Earth by Sheila Hamanaka
Rich oil paintings explore the diversity of the world's ethnic heritages. For students in kindergarten to fourth grade.

Me and Uncle Romie: A Story Inspired by the Life and Art of Romare Bearden by Claire Hartflied
Written for children ages 6 to 10. Fictional account of the life of Romare Bearden told through his nephew's eyes. Illustrated in the Bearden style.

Quilted Landscape: Conversations With Young Immigrants by Yale Strom
Interviews about what's its like to be an immigrant in America with young people from 26 different countries (interviewed before 9-11-01). Printed like a teen magazine with black/white photographs. For grades 5 and up.

Romare Bearden: Collage of Memories by Jan Greenberg
Large-format introduction to Bearden's work. Accessible poetry for students in grades 5 and 6.

Vocabulary List

Use this list to explore new vocabulary, create idea webs, or brainstorm related subjects.

African-American
Artist
Authentic
Bearden
Blues
Clothes/clothing
Collage
Contemporary
Culture
Cut
Dolls
Diverse/diversity
Dress
Era
Ethnicity
Fabric
Figures

Glue
Harlem
Heritage
Immigrant
Jazz
Paste
Renaissance
Romare
Setting
Social change
Time period
Traditional
Unify

Artwork by students from St. Theresa School, Hellertown, Pennsylvania.

Artwork by students from CS 102,
Bronx, New York.
Teacher: Neila Steiner

Artwork by students from
St. Theresa School,
Hellertown, Pennsylvania.

What Does It Mean?

Abstract: art that emphasizes line, color, and general
or geometric forms and how they relate to one another;
20th century art was often abstract

Accordion-style fold: folding paper pleats so the paper
springs open and closed

Collage: art composed by attaching on a single surface
various materials not typically associated with one another

Symbols: image that represents an idea or object

We Are the Children

	K-2	3-4	5-6
Suggested Preparation and Discussion	Display photography, books, and dolls that show and describe traditional and contemporary authentic dress (both everyday and special occasion) from various cultures. Make sure that many depict cultures with which the students are familiar, including their families. Students identify an ethnic group within their families or community to depict in traditional clothing.	Display photographs, books, or dolls that show and describe traditional and contemporary authentic dress. Make a list to identify similarities and differences among at least three cultures including those of families in the community. Discuss how Romare Bearden created people and scenes. Talk about the variety of mediums he used, including fabric, paper, photographs, and paint. Examine how these materials are cut, arranged, and glued together to create new designs. Students each select two or three ethnicities to portray in collage. Research traditional designs, customs, indigenous food, shelter, and other unique qualities of the chosen groups. Especially note clothing and how it has changed over time.	

Discuss how and why people around the world dress differently—both daily and for special occasions. Ask students to share any experiences that they have wearing traditional clothing that reflects their family heritage.

Study Romare Bearden's collages. What do students notice about the people's clothing? About the setting and time period in which they are depicted?

Crayola® Supplies	• Colored Pencils • Crayons • Glitter Glue • Glue Sticks • Markers • Paint Brushes • Scissors • Tempera Paint
Other Materials	• Collage materials • Construction paper • Craft paper • Fabric scraps • Oak tag • Recycled gift wrap • Recycled magazines • Recycled newspapers • Water containers • White paper
Set-up/Tips	• Cover painting surface with newspaper. • Create several templates of human figures for children to trace around if they choose.

Dolls
Private Collection.

1. African Ndebele Initiation Doll
Artist unknown
Beads, felt, leather, wood and wire
4" x 3 1/2" x 10 1/2"

2. Japanese Wood Puzzle Doll
Artist unknown
Wood, paint
2" x 2" x 3 1/2"

3. Seminole Indian Doll
Artist unknown
Beads, cotton fabric, threads, coconut fiber
5 1/4" x 3 1/2" x 1 1/2"

4. Northwest Alaskan Doll
Artist unknown
Ceramic, metal, paint
2" x 1 1/2" x 3 1/2"

5. Japanese Paper Maché Doll
Artist unknown
Paper, paint, bamboo, gold leaf
7" x 5 1/2" x 5 1/2"

	K-2	3-4	5-6
Process: Session 1 20-30 min.	**Paint mural** 1. Outline continents on large craft paper. Paint in ocean and landmass areas. Air-dry the map.	**Prepare the collage setting** 1. Students choose patterned paper, fabric scraps, and other materials to develop an authentic time-period background setting for each of their collages. Include details such as clothing, furnishings, and shelter.	
Process: Session 2 15-20 min.	**Create figures** 2. On oak tag, students draw a human figure with arms reaching out to the sides, or trace around the template. 3. Cut out figures.	**Create figures** 2. Fold construction paper in half, (joining short ends). Fold top edge back to the crease. Turn paper over and fold on opposite side to complete accordion fold. 3. With accordion in vertical position, draw simple figures on top of the folds. Make sure that hands and feet extend to the edges. Cut out figures.	**Create figures** 2. In the style of Romare Bearden's collages, cut out bodies, authentic clothing styles, facial features, and other design elements from recycled papers or fabric. Glue figures to collage backgrounds. 3. Enhance collage elements using crayon, marker, and/or paint.
Process: Session 3 20-30 min.	**Decorate figures** 4. Cut and glue facial features from recycled magazines on figures in the style of Romare Bearden's collages. 5. Color, cut out, and glue decorative paper or fabric scraps to replicate authentic clothing styles from various cultures and time periods. Enrich designs with markers, crayons, and/or glitter glue. 6. Display paper figures in a unified manner.		**Display collages** 4. Students write short descriptive paragraphs detailing the culture and time period depicted in each collage. 5. Display the collages in a way that unifies students' diverse works.
Assessment	• Students represent a human figure with detailed facial and clothing features. • Students identify the culture of their figures and describe the distinctive elements of their authentic clothing designs.		• Verify accuracy of students' research as reflected in the figures' clothing and background for the collage. • Are collages detailed and aesthetically pleasing? • Do written descriptions match the clothing and settings depicted in the collages?
	• Ask students to reflect on this lesson and write a DREAM statement to summarize the most important things they learned.		
Extensions	Go on a collage hunt. Collect examples of collage design in books, magazines, and on TV. Read more of the storybooks of Romare Bearden. What other fine artists have illustrated children's books (Jean-Paul Basquait and William Steif, for example)? Cutting oak tag may be difficult for younger children and some with motor disabilities. Pair children with an older student or ask for volunteers to assist.	Connect with students from other parts of the world, such as adopting sister schools or communicating with pen pals. Research and adopt an interesting, fun, and safe program. Brainstorm ways that ethnic clothing can be preserved for future generations to see and understand. How could it be shown in the context of an event? Review local newspapers for examples of diversity in the community. Look for coverage of pow-wows, religious holidays, and other events in which people wear traditional dress.	Students review Bearden's work and identify elements that speak to social issues of his time. Listen to jazz and blues recordings that Bearden might have heard. Share the connections between the music and his art. Examine other artists who they have been influenced by musical forms like Robert Rauschenberg by John Cage or Andy Warhol by pop music. Ask gifted students to find contemporary art that carries a message of social change. Why does the artist feel compelled to address issues through art? How effective is art in getting the message across?

Crayola **Dream~Makers** Building fun and creativity into standards-based learning

Action Makes Dreams Come True

Objectives

Students identify a social issue that needs to be addressed either locally, in their state, nationally, or internationally.

Students create "Action Makes Dreams Come True" containers in which to collect, analyze, and present suggested concrete, practical solutions from classmates.

Multiple Intelligences

Interpersonal   Logical-mathematical

National Standards

Visual Arts Standard #6
Making connections between visual arts and other disciplines

Social Studies Standard #10
Civic Ideals and Practices—experiences that provide for the study of the ideas, principles, and practices of citizenship in a democratic republic.

Health Education Standard #8
Students will demonstrate the ability to advocate for personal, family, and community health.

Background Information

Native American crafters create objects called dream-catchers. It is believed by some that hanging the dream-catcher in and around living spaces will enable the catcher to catch people's bad dreams.

Other cultures believe that putting dreams in boxes will help dreamers capture their dreams. A Native American legend about a dream box states that if you put your dream in a box, hold it before you go to bed, and wish with all your heart for it to come true, when you get up in the morning, your dream will come true.

It is hard for scientists to study dreams while people are sleeping. No one can be forced to dream nor can one influence what is dreamt about, plus there is no way to verify what is actually dreamed because scientists would only learn what the dreamer remembers about the dream. Some people believe that if you don't write down what you dream within minutes after you wake in the morning, you will forget the dream.

Resources

Freedom's Children: Young Civil Rights Activists Tell Their Own Stories by Ellen Levine
The title says it all. Lots of historic photographs illustrate this history of the recent past in the United States. Stories inspire upper elementary and middle school students to wonder what they would have done in the same situation, and dream about what they can do today.

Going Green: A Kid's Handbook to Saving the Planet by John Elkington
A cartoon handbook for fourth to eighth graders. Contains success stories and numerous statistical sidebars. Offers many suggestions of actions for young people to take to save the planet.

Harvesting Hope: The Story of Cesar Chavez by Kathleen Krull
Although it is in a picture book format, the material covered is appropriate for students starting in second grade. It focuses on one event in the long battle for migrant workers' rights, with Chavez at the center.

Martin's Big Words: The Life of Dr. Martin Luther King, Jr. by Doreen Rappaport
Using King's original words to tell the powerful story of his life, collage illustrations dramatically complement this picture book. A listing of important dates in Dr. King's life is useful for elementary students.

Vocabulary List

Use this list to explore new vocabulary, create idea webs, or brainstorm related subjects.

Action	Migrant farm workers
Activist	National
Change	Opportunity
Citizen	Outline
Civic	Protect
Civil rights	Protest
Common good	Responsibility
Community	Rights
Democracy/democratic	Shape
Focal point	Social change
Emphasis	Support
Equal	Unity
Equality	Vote/voter
Global	Workers
Grass roots	
Ideal	
Informed	
Justice	
Leader	
Local	

What Does It Mean?

Advocate: stand up for an idea or position

Dream-catcher: Native American hoop with a spider-web design inside intended to filter out bad dreams

Focal point: primary area of interest in a work of art

	K-2	3-4	5-6
Suggested Preparation and Discussion	Display books and posters of individuals who identified and worked to correct social concerns. Two examples are Cesar Chavez, who helped U.S. migrant farm workers get better working conditions, and the Rev. Dr. Martin Luther King, Jr. who worked for civil rights for African Americans. Discuss what elements make a visual statement. What catches the eye and demands attention? Discuss how the use of a focal point, color, and bold images (emphasis) translate to conveying a message on a box top. Display books and posters of individuals who identified and worked to correct social concerns. Children each research and choose a social issue as a theme for their "Action Makes Dreams Come True" boxes.		
	Read *Martin's Big Words* or a similar book about an advocate for change. Introduce other individuals who changed the country or the world for the better. Discuss social change and how people's dreams helped shape the way we live today.	Do you ever dream about a world where problems were solved and things were different? What makes changes happen? Who starts those changes rolling? Introduce individuals who changed the country or the world for the better. Discuss social change and how people's dreams helped shape the way we live today.	Ask students if they were in charge of things, what would be different? Think BIG, think real, and think important. How can you turn those dreams into action so flawed social situations and issues are improved? Study biographies of individuals who changed the country or the world for the better. Discuss social change and how people's dreams helped shape the way we live today.
Crayola® Supplies	• Colored Pencils • Glue Sticks • Oil Pastels • School Glue • Scissors		
Other Materials	• Construction paper • Recycled boxes with lids • Ribbon or yarn (optional) • White paper		
Set-up/Tips	• Ask parent volunteers to collect recycled ribbon and small boxes with lids.		

Decorative Boxes
Artist unknown
Private Collection.

	K-2	3-4	5-6
Process: Session 1 20-30 min.	**Create action boxes** 1. Trace around the box lid on white paper. Cut around the outlined shape. 2. Sketch ideas that illustrate the identified social problem. 3. Fill in ideas using oil pastels. Select colors and shapes that emphasize the social issue. 4. Glue finished design to box lid. Air-dry the glue. 5. Decorate or cover the box sides with construction paper to create a unified presentation.		
Process: Session 2 20-30 min.	**Partner to find solutions** 6. With a partner, pick another student's box and talk about the problem identified. 7. Brainstorm several solutions. 8. Draw and/or write solution ideas on paper. Older students and adults can assist emerging writers.	**Design solution scrolls** 6. Display and review each classmate's box and its social issue. 7. Write solutions on paper scrolls. Roll into cylinder and tie with ribbon or yarn. 8. Place solutions in appropriate boxes.	
Process: Session 3 20-30 min.	**Review solutions** 9. Share ideas with class about how to solve the problem identified by each box.	**Review solution scrolls** 9. Box creators review ideas presented in their boxes. 10. Creators choose the three best solution scroll choices to share orally with the class.	
Assessment	• Children can identify, understand, and offer solutions to issues raised by classmates. • Children clearly present possible solutions to classmates.	• Children can identify, understand, and offer solutions to issues raised by classmates. • Do solutions on scrolls indicate that students understand issues at stake?	• Children can identify, understand, and offer solutions to issues raised by classmates. • Are solutions creative and realistic? Did students present them to classmates clearly?
	• Ask students to reflect on this lesson and write a DREAM statement to summarize the most important things they learned.		
Extensions	Pick one solution and draw it in detail. Identify and embrace a classroom issue. Plan and implement action. Students with special needs may benefit from small group discussion on each issue and possible solutions.	Listen to Dr. King's "I Have a Dream" speech. Ask children to write or present a similar message in their own words. Create a list of women who have made a difference in everyday life. Research each to learn more about women's history. Gifted students research the feasibility of the solutions found in their boxes and present the best choices.	Vote to choose the most doable solution to one issue. Make a class commitment to carry out action. Break the plan into small, doable steps. Develop a timeline. Follow through with action.

Decorative Boxes
Artist unknown
Private Collection.

Noticeable Norens—Make Certain It Is on the Curtain

Objectives

Students identify the roles of markets as providers of goods and services in various levels of economic and commerce systems.

Students create team norens (Japanese-style curtains) containing symbols and signs to advertise an imaginary local, regional, national, or international business and its products or services.

Multiple Intelligences

Interpersonal
Linguistic
Spatial

National Standards

Visual Arts Standard #6
Making connections between visual arts and other disciplines

Social Studies Standard #7
Production, Distribution, and Consumption—experiences that provide for the study of how people organize for the production, distribution, and consumption of goods and services.

Social Studies Standard #9
Global connections—experiences that provide for the study of global connections and interdependence.

Health Education Standard #2
Students will analyze the influence of family, peers, culture, media, technology and other factors on health behaviors.

Background Information

The English translation of noren is "shop curtain." In Japan, norens hang in the doors of storefronts, advertising what products and services are available inside. The art of making these shop curtains originally involved a tie-dying process done by hand. Shopkeepers carefully pick designs for their norens because it is the first thing that greets visitors who enter their businesses.

Just as norens are a popular art form in Japan, advertising remains an art form all over the world. Savvy graphic designers and business owners create universally recognized symbols and designs to attract customers.

Resources

I Live in Tokyo by Mari Takabayashi
Told from a first-person perspective for kindergartens through second graders. Shares what it is like to live in a Japanese city with watercolor pictures. Includes a glossary of Japanese words.

Japan for Kids: The Ultimate Guide for Parents and Their Children by Diane Wiltshire
Travel book that presents a realistic, non-stereotypical picture of Japanese activities and occasions.

Made You Look: How Advertising Works and Why You Should Know by Shari Graydon
A hip insider overview of the advertising industry. Thought provoking for 5th and 6th graders. Deconstructs an ad campaign.

Pictorial Encyclopedia of Japanese Life and Events by Gakken Staff
A visual compendium of all things Japanese.

Vocabulary List

Use this list to explore new vocabulary, create idea webs, or brainstorm related subjects.

Ad/advertise/advertising
Balance
Business
Campaign
Commerce
Curtain
Economics
Emphasis
Font
Goods
Hanging
Image
International
Japan
Japanese
Line
Local
Logo
Market
National
Noren
Pattern
Products
Promote
Promotion
Regional
Services
Shape
Shop
Sign
Unity

What Does It Mean?

Elements: in art the elements are line, shape, color, texture, pattern etcetera

Symbol: use of an image to represent an idea or object

Artwork by students from Jordan Community School, Chicago, Illinois.
Teacher: Elyse Martin

thes for Special Occasions

assion For Fashion

International Clothing Co.

INTERNATIONAL JUMP ROPING COMPANY

SALES OF SPECIAL EQUIPMENT FOR EVERYONE

ALL WELCOME

Artwork by students from St. Theresa School, Hellertown, Pennsylvania.

Crayola Dream~Makers
Building fun and creativity into standards-based learning

	K-2	3-4	5-6
Suggested Preparation and Discussion	Display business logos from recycled magazines, empty product packages, and other sources. Why do businesses use logos in their advertising? What other techniques do they use to attract buyers to their products and services? What are "goods and services?" Look at examples of Japanese norens. Talk about their function in advertising Japanese businesses.		
	Ask students to bring in examples of logos with which they are familiar. Why do logos make a product stand out? Discuss the idea of a business logo. Talk about team mascots as logos for a school. Talk about what colors are most eye-catching.	Ask students to define advertising. What types of advertising appeal most to children? To adults? Why? What goods and services are typically advertised in your area of the United States? What other goods and services might be more suitable in other states or countries? Why? Consider whether heavy winter clothes would be sold on tropical islands, for example. Share ideas about the elements of a successful, memorable logo, sign, or symbol. Talk about what design qualities make a good logo.	

Crayola® Supplies
- Colored Pencils   • Fabric Markers
- Glitter Glue   • School Glue   • Scissors

Other Materials
- Rulers   • White cotton fabric
- White paper   • Yarn or ribbon

Set-up/Tips
- Younger children and some students with special needs may prefer to work on smaller pieces of fabric.
- Ask an adult to iron freezer paper to back of fabric to stabilize it before decorating (optional).

Historic Sun Inn Advertising Sign
Bethlehem, Pennsylvania
Photo by R. De Long

Japanese Children's
Day Banners
Circa 1960
Artist unknown
Dyed cotton fabric
Japan
Private Collection.

	K-2	3-4	5-6

Process:
Session 1
20-30 min.

Invent a business and logo

1. Divide into small groups to brainstorm ideas. Invent a business name and product/service that the group would like to advertise.

2. Design logo and visuals that identify the business's service and/or product. Sketch ideas for symbols, colors, fonts, and other elements of a logo. Keep in mind the size of the fabric and proportions of the various elements.

Process:
Session 2
15-20 min.

Create noren

3. Decide on best design to advertise the imaginary business. Which design makes the strongest statement? Emphasizes the product most? Make sure the final design catches the eye. How well does it visually illustrate the business's purpose with color, pattern, image, shape, and line? Strive to achieve balance and unity within the design.

4. Draw the final advertisement on a cloth panel. Add eye-catching elements to complete the overall effect.

Process:
Session 3
20-30 min.

Display noren

5. Roll paper into tight cylinder as long as the width of the noren. Glue down free edge. Glue noren to cylinder. Hold until glue is set.

6. Thread ribbon through cylinder for hanging.

Assessment

- Students work cooperatively to invent a business and develop an eye-catching, balanced logo and ad. The product/service promoted on noren is identifiable.
- Design visually relates to name and business advertised.
- Ask students to reflect on this lesson and write a DREAM statement to summarize the most important things they learned.

Extensions

Design a class logo. Create accompanying stationery, signs, business cards, and other materials.

Discover more about Japanese culture. What clothes are traditional in the country? What do most people wear now? What foods are common? If possible, interview someone who has lived in Japan.

Encourage children with motor disabilities to design their norens with computer-assisted technology.

Visit a Japanese business, store, or restaurant to see norens. Look for other unique cultural elements such as the welcoming cat statue called Maneki Neko. Make one with Crayola Model Magic® compound. See the Welcoming Cat Sculpture on Crayola.com.

Interview a local business owner. How was the product and/or service chosen? Who are the primary customers? How does the business reach them?

Make norens for classrooms, administration offices, and other areas within the school.

Gifted children may be interested in exploring more about the Japanese economy. What products from Japan are well known in the United States? Why?

Learn how to draw in Manga or Anime style. What design elements are most prominent in this popular Japanese art form?

Restaurant Noren
Osaka, Japan
Photo by R. De Long

Buckingham Palace Gate
Royal Coat of Arms
London, England
Photo by R. De Long

Interactive Timeline

Objectives

Students develop a three-dimensional, interactive timeline that illustrates events from history (3-6) or their daily life (K-2).

Students render the abstract concept of historical time into an assemblage of visual symbols and 3-dimensional objects.

Multiple Intelligences

Linguistic
Spatial

What Does It Mean?

Abstract: art that emphasizes line, color, and general or geometric forms and how they relate to one another; 20th century art was often abstract

Assemblage: unified sculpture that combines unrelated objects

Installation: a contemporary style of exhibiting media within a 3-D environment, indoors and outdoors, often in large scale

National Standards

Visual Arts Standard #3	Social Studies Standard #2
Choosing and evaluating a range of subject matter, symbols, and ideas	Time, Continuity, and Change—experiences that provide for the study of ways human being view themselves in and over time.
	Health Education Standard #3 Students will demonstrate the ability to access valid information and products and services to enhance health.

Background Information

With growing accessibility to the World Wide Web, the tool of the timeline has deepened and expanded. There are timelines for numerous topics from art to religion to science and math. The Web has enabled the "line" in timeline to transform into a multi-dimensional shape and a very useful device. At www.hyperhistory.com, for example, more than 2,000 files are interconnected to portray an expansive overview of historical events.

In 1955, Rosa Parks sat in an empty bus seat, an action that eventually made her a key symbol of the Civil Rights Movement. By 1961, activists and supporters of civil rights in the United States realized that segregation on interstate buses was unconstitutional. Activists organized Freedom Riders to travel throughout the South on buses in an effort to force the John F. Kennedy administration to support the civil rights movement and end segregation. The violence these activists met did not deter them from their work. Finally, under pressure from Attorney General Robert Kennedy, the Interstate Commerce Commission ruled to outlaw segregation on the interstate buses.

Simple timelines can be made that show people, places and events that occurs in the daily life of a person.

Resources

All in a Day by Mitsumasa Anno
Ten international artists illustrate a child's day. Features eight different parts of the world.

If You Give a Mouse a Cookie by Laura Joffe Numeroff
Classic cause-and-effect story told with sweet humor and colorful pictures. For young children.

Timetables of History: A Horizontal Linkage of People and Events by Bernard Grun
Reference book for older elementary students. Provides various examples of timelines and the linkage between them.

Vocabulary List

Use this list to explore new vocabulary, create idea webs, or brainstorm related subjects.

Cause
Collage
Day
Effect
Events
Facts
Form
Historical
History
Installation
Interactive
Line
Model

Replica
Represent
Result
Schedule
Sequence
Three-dimensional
Time
Visual symbols

Scrapbooks of Maura Weins
Artist: Maura Weins
Collection of Maura Weins.

Artwork by students from
Mt. Prospect Elementary School,
Basking Ridge, New Jersey.
Teachers: Susan Bivona
           Regina De Francisco

	K-2	3-4	5-6
Suggested Preparation and Discussion	Ask students to think about the routines in their daily lives. In what order do they do things? Do they put on their pants before taking off their pjs? Demonstrate how to make a 3-D timeline by using classroom routines as an example. If possible, incorporate digital pictures. Ask children to choose a day during the next week to represent in a 3-D timeline. Suggest they use a journal to jot down everything they do on that day. Ask them to write approximate times when they accomplished each task. Encourage the use of photography to document their activities.	Discuss the statement "History is a sequence of events." One way of looking at the past is to examine the factors that led up to an occurrence. This may be graphically represented in a timeline, where successive elements are displayed in an order within a particular historical period. Conduct an in-depth exploration of a historical event that is meaningful to children, such as the U.S. Civil Rights Movement in the 1950s and 1960s. The bus ride that Rosa Parks took in 1955 in Montgomery, Alabama, lends itself well to chronological analysis. Collect pictures and news clippings that illustrate the events. Find photographs of the people and places involved in the period. Arrange them in chronological order. Depending on the event chosen and information collected, small-group work may be an effective organizational strategy.	

Display samples of timelines in various formats and covering different time periods and types of events.
Display samples of collages, such as the work of Romare Bearden.

Crayola® Supplies	• Colored Pencils • Markers • Model Magic® • Paint Brushes • School Glue • Scissors • Watercolors
Other Materials	• Construction paper • Containers of water • Corrugated cardboard • Craft materials • Paper • Recycled boxes • Recycled magazines • Recycled newspaper
Set-up/Tips	• Consider using a large sheet of corrugated cardboard as a sturdy base for the installation. Request a large appliance box from a store and cut it to size. • Cover the painting surface with newspaper.

Artwork by students from
College Oaks Elementary School,
Lake Charles, Louisiana.
Teacher: Bobbi Yancey

	K-2	3-4	5-6

Process: Session 1 20-30 min.

K-2	3-4
Outline the sequence	**Outline the sequence**
1. Ask children to sketch objects and people to represent each event in their day.	1. List key events on slips of paper. Choose the most important ones to depict in the installation.
2. Choose at least five key events to portray in chronological order.	2. Arrange these events in chronological order.
3. Decide which models, replicas, news clippings, photographs, and symbols to use to represent each event.	3. Decide which models, replicas, news clippings, photographs, and symbols to use to represent each event.

Process: Session 2 30-45 min.

Design collage timeline

4. Cover cardboard with construction paper. Write the title on the base.

5. Sketch the shape of the timeline. It might be a straight line, but could also be a clock, a path or street, or a graph. Note where photos, drawings, news stories, and 3-D objects will be placed along the line.

6. Use Model Magic to sculpt the 3-D replicas that symbolize events. These could range from a toothbrush for young children to the Lincoln Memorial for a civil rights presentation. Air-dry the sculptures for at least 24 hours.

Process: Session 3 (optional) 20-30 min.

Paint sculptures

7. If children used white Model Magic compound, paint sculptures with watercolors. Use very little water for the most intense hues. Air-dry the paint overnight.

Process: Session 4 20-30 min.

Assemble timeline

8. Glue replicas in place on timeline base.

9. Attach other items in collage-style along timeline. Add labels and other decorative elements as needed.

Assessment

K-2	3-4
• Timeline depicts accurate sequencing of at least five events in daily life.	• Important historical data and symbols of key events are represented in sequence.
• Symbols chosen to represent routines clearly communicate to viewers.	• The timeline is creatively constructed in a way that incorporates meaningful symbols and 3-D objects.

• Ask students to reflect on this lesson and write a DREAM statement to summarize the most important things they learned.

Extensions

K-2	3-4
Watch video series *Families of the World* to follow other children's days from all around the world. Ask children to identify everyday activities that are similar and different among students. Children could even interview each other and compare their daily routines. When do they get up? What do they eat for breakfast? Consider asking younger students and those with some types of disabilities to work with their families to prepare a timeline of daily routines.	Discuss other approaches to the study of history in non-chronological order, without being concerned about the sequence of events. This is an especially important method when studying the history of everyday life and everyday people who don't have big events in their lives but are nevertheless part of history. Prepare an installation for a community facility on a topic of interest. For example, trace the inventions that resulted in book printing to display in a library. Gifted students could research events around the world in a given time period. Compile them in a vertical timeline. They might, for example, find out what was happening during the decade in which they or their parents were born.

Protect an Invention

Objectives

Students explore the patent process for awarding property rights in the United States.

Students create a miniature model of an invention and present an oral or written description of how it works and will benefit society. In the process, they grasp how the creative processes of art and invention involve similar problem-solving skills.

Multiple Intelligences

Interpersonal
Logical-mathematical
Spatial

What Does It Mean?

Armature: a skeletal framework or support on which a sculpture is constructed in clay, wax, plaster, or other media

Form: 3-dimensional figure (length, width, depth)

National Standards

Visual Arts Standard #1 Understanding and applying media, techniques, and processes	**Social Studies Standard #8** Science, Technology, and Society—experiences that provide for the study of global connections and interdependence.
	Health Education Standard #3 Students will demonstrate the ability to access valid information and products and services to enhance health.

Background Information

A patent for an invention is a grant of property right by the United States government to the inventor, through the U.S. Patent and Trademark Office. When someone is issued a patent they are given the right to exclude others from making, using, or selling the invention that was patented. There are three types of patents. The first kind is given for the plans designed around how an invention works. The second type is for unique designs in appearance of an invention and the third is for living plants. A patent usually last 20 years and takes an average of 22 months to be granted.

A copyright provides protection to works of authorship and lasts the life of the author plus 70 years. A trademark is a word, name, symbol, or device that distinguishes it from the goods of others. Trademarks may be renewed forever.

Resources

Brainstorm! Stories of 20 American Kid Inventors
by Tom Tucker
Detailed portraits of diverse kid inventors. For students starting in fifth grade. One chapter explains the patent and copyright process with advice to beginning inventors.

Imaginative Inventions by Charise Mericle Harper
Real facts about inventions presented whimsically with doggerel verse and zany illustrations. For children 5 to 8 years old.

The New Way Things Work by David Macaulay
Classic reference book contains clearly written and expertly illustrated explanations of how most things work. Includes up-to-date items like iPods and CD burners with the help of a humorous mammoth.

Unuseless Japanese Inventions by Kenji Kawakami
Inspires funky, although practical, inventions. Filled with photographs of real inventions made by everyday people to solve common issues in Japan.

Vocabulary List

Use this list to explore new vocabulary, create idea webs, or brainstorm related subjects.

Benefit/beneficial
Copyright
Creation
Creative
Develop
Form
Function
Government
Idea
Invention
Inventor
Innovation
Legal
Model

New
Patent
Problem-solving
Process
Property right
Science
Technology
Trademark
Unique

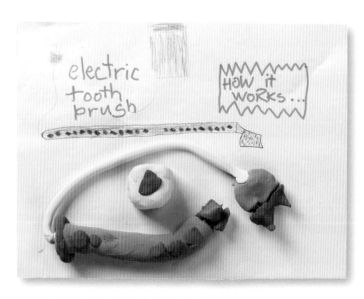

Artwork by students from St. Theresa School, Hellertown, Pennsylvania.

The visulizer This invention uses up absolutly no electricity what so ever, It runs on solar power and vinagar battery. When you you [et] home the tape player reminds you of things you've forgotten, If turns on your computer and even turns off your slow cooker so you can eat right away. The cost off your electric bill [...] more forgetting [...] since it uses no [...] bill goes down. It [...] time you don't [...]

Draw a sketch of the invention/innovation in the rectangle.

turning on computer

Artwork by students from
Maple Avenue Middle School,
Littlestown, Pennsylvania.
Teacher: Pam Gall

Tyler 6-red,A.

My invention is a water Purifier. It is
A box in your base-ment that gets the water
when you drain your sink and bath tub.
When water travels down the Pipe, it goes
into the Purifier and cleans the water.
when the clean water is Finished, that
water travels through another Pipe
to a boiler witch heats up half of the
water.
This benefits sircoly by never having
to Pay your hot water ever again because
t-maker Drinkable, but water that from any
bath tub, or any sink in your home

1st Floor

Bathroom

BASEMENT

Draw a sketch of the invention/innovation in the...

Crayola

Dream~Makers®
Building fun and creativity into standards-based learning

Protect an Invention

	K-2	3-4	5-6

Suggested Preparation and Discussion

Display photographs and examples of major inventions. Highlight inventors who have advanced society with their creative thinking, such as Leonardo da Vinci.

Ask students to identify inventions that they see as valuable. Trace the development of a common invention from its early prototype to current model, such as the sewing machine invented by Elias Howe.

Discuss the process that inventors often follow, from identifying a problem through research and testing to application for a patent and manufacturing. If possible, ask a local inventor to talk with the group about the entire process.

Research how ideas and inventions are protected by patents or copyrights in the United States.

Crayola® Supplies

• Colored Pencils   • Glitter Glue   • Model Magic®   • School Glue   • Scissors

Other Materials

• Decorative craft materials   • Modeling tools   • Recycled boxes   • Recycled cardboard   • White paper

Set-up/Tips

• Ask families to donate cardboard gift-wrap rolls, small boxes, scraps of ribbon and fabric, and other items to use as armatures and embellishments for art projects such as this one.

• Demonstrate common sculpting techniques to children such as joining, impressing, and the use of armatures.

United States Patent Award Plaques
Patents awarded to Karen M. Mariano,
Richard E. Miller, Robert C. Dereamus
for innovative product design
7 1/2" x 11 1/2"
Collection of Crayola LLC.

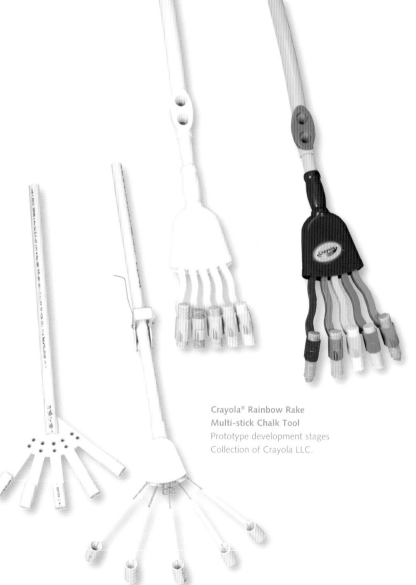

Crayola® Rainbow Rake
Multi-stick Chalk Tool
Prototype development stages
Collection of Crayola LLC.

	K-2	3-4	5-6

Process: Session 1 20-30 min.

Brainstorm ideas

1. In small groups or individually, students imagine a new invention that would help the world. What would it do? What would it look like? What technology would it use? What is new about it?

2. Sketch ideas on paper. Add concrete details. Choose one invention to develop.

Process: Session 2 15-20 min.

Build model

3. Working with Model Magic® compound, construct a detailed miniature model of the invention using the sketch for reference. Use armatures as needed.

4. Attach and embed decorative craft materials to embellish the invention. Add glitter glue highlights.

5. Air-dry the invention for 24 hours.

Process: Session 3 20-30 min.

Present the invention

6. Students orally describe to class how their inventions work and why they are helpful to people. They explain what is unique about them so that they could be patented.

Present the invention

6. Write accompanying explanatory text with diagrams to show how the invention works. Include a one-paragraph description explaining how the invention will benefit society.

7. Display inventions in a public area for others to appreciate.

Assessment

- Did children follow the invention process from ideation to sketches to modeling?
- Students clearly describe how their inventions work and the problems they address.

- Did students follow the steps in the invention process? If they worked together, did they do so cooperatively? Does the invention address a need?
- Prepare a simplified patent form. Ask for information about the invention's function, form, use of technology, and evidence that the idea is unique. Students fill it out with clear details about their inventions.

- Ask students to reflect on this lesson and write a DREAM statement to summarize the most important things they learned.

Extensions

Ask children to take an inventory of their favorite household inventions such as dishwashers or timers on lights. Why did they choose these items?

Discuss what life would be like without inventions such as telephones and cars.

Students with some disabilities may find it helpful to use computers to sketch and even model their inventions. Suggest that they invent something that would make their lives more comfortable.

Visit a historic site interpreting early American life. Focus on inventions since that time.

Find out information about inventors. What challenges did the Wright brothers, for example, encounter along the way?

Interview parents and grand-parents about an invention that was new during their lifetimes. Which invention changed the world the most? Debate findings.

Discuss how advances in science and technology enable change. Consider the impact of the invention of the cotton gin by Eli Whitney, for example, or Stephanie Kwolek, inventor of Kevlar®.

Identify inventions that are helpful and harmful to society. What inventions were thought impossible 20 or 100 years ago?

Suggest that gifted students trace the impact of one invention on another. For example, Teflon® was initially invented for the U.S. space program. What other inventions did that lead to?

Ask children to consider: What encourages creativity? What dampens it? Share how you are inspired and what tramps on your creativity.

Coat finished invention with glaze of equal parts or water and school glue for added protection. Cover art surface with recycled newspaper first. Air-dry the glaze before handling.

Time to Cool Down Fans

Objectives

Students reflect on and practice decision-making processes that enable them to identify situations and implement self-disciplined strategies to defuse volatile situations.

Students use art elements, symbols, and words to reflect their self-control strategies on Time to Cool Down Fans.

Multiple Intelligences

Interpersonal
Intrapersonal
Linguistic

What Does It Mean?

Elements: lines, shapes, colors, texture, pattern that are included in making any artwork

Harmonious: pleasing, consistent design

Unified/unity: all the parts in a work are harmonious and appear to be complete, one area does not stand out over another

National Standards

Visual Arts Standard #1	Social Studies Standard #5
Understanding and apply media, techniques, and processes	Individuals, Groups, and Institutions—experiences that provide for the study of interactions among individuals, groups, and institutions.
	Health Education Standard #4 Students will demonstrate the ability to use interpersonal communication skills to enhance health and avoid or reduce health risks.

Background Information

In ancient Egypt, the design of hand fans often imitated leaf fronds of the blue lotus or date palm tree. Because fans move air, the symbol of a fan came to represent breath and ultimately life and the giving of life itself. Surviving examples of fan-bearers holding semicircular fans on long poles have been found on the walls of many tombs including that of Tutankhamen (1350 BCE).

Thousands of years later, in the eighteenth century, during the height of fan usage in Europe and America, a secret language of fan was practiced. How a lady's fan was held—was it closed, half-opened, and how it was presented to a gentleman—all sent nonverbal messages to those in the know. Today hand-held fans are used as advertising surfaces.

Resources

A Volcano in My Tummy: Helping Children to Handle Anger by Eliane Whitehouse
For ages 6 to 13. Teaches anger management skills through stories, activities, and games.

Novelty Hand Fans: Fashionable, Functional, Fun Accessories of the Past by Cynthia and Michael Fendel
Information and beautiful photographs of hand fans throughout time.

The Magic Fan by Keith Baker
Storybook about empowerment for kindergartners through second graders. Bold illustrations in the shape of a folding fan.

Vocabulary List

Use this list to explore new vocabulary, create idea webs, or brainstorm related subjects.

Anger
Behavior
Breathe
Calm down
Chill out
Conflict
Control
Cool down
Count
Emotions
Fan
Handle
Harmonious
Management
Pattern
Resolution
Self-control
Self-discipline
Strategy
Unity
Volatile

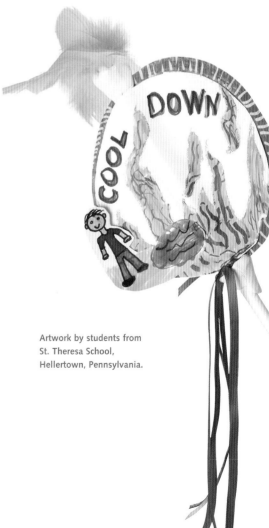

Artwork by students from
St. Theresa School,
Hellertown, Pennsylvania.

Artwork by students from
Governor Wolf Elementary School,
Bethlehem, Pennsylvania.
Teacher: Patricia Check

	K-2	3-4	5-6
Suggested Preparation and Discussion	Ask students how they typically react when someone makes them angry or does something with which they don't agree. How did they feel afterwards? What would have happened if they had counted to 10 first? What other strategies would help them to remember to pause before reacting?	Discuss with students how often they think that their immediate reaction to situations is the best reaction. Talk about examples and the consequences. Explore situations that call for thinking responses vs. those that require prompt reactions. Share strategies for cooling down when emotions get too hot.	Talk about how situations can be made better or worse by people's reactions to them. Share examples from real and fictional circumstances. Discuss tools students can use to help them evaluate a situation before reacting.
	Students identify fan shapes and colors that could remind them to calm down before reacting to volatile situations.		
Crayola® Supplies	• Colored Pencils • Markers • School Glue • Scissors		
Other Materials	• Decorative craft items • Drawing paper • Oak tag • Rubber bands • Yarn		
Set-up/Tips	• Place a large book on top of glued fans during final drying time.		

Indonesian, Chinese, African, and Spanish Fans
20th Century
Handpainted wood, sandalwood, silk, paper, grasses
Approximate height 8"
Collection of R. De Long and Sandra Lee Wood.

Process: **Session 1** **30-45 min.**	**Design fans** 1. Cut out two large, identical paper fan shapes that represent calming symbols. 2. Sketch designs on both fans with colored pencils. Include words to help calm their emotions such as "Chill Out." Suggest that students use cool colors and soothing patterns to achieve harmonious unity in their designs. 3. Color fans with markers.
Process: **Session 2** **15-20 min.**	**Produce handle** 4. Tightly roll paper into fan handles. 5. Glue the tube's outside edge. Wrap rubber bands around handles while glue dries. 6. Wrap and glue yarn around half of the handle. Cut and glue fringe to bottoms of handles. Air-dry the glue.
Process: **Session 3** **30-45 min.**	**Assemble fan** 7. Spread glue on the back of one fan shape. 8. Place handle on top so that the decorated half hangs out. 9. Apply decorative elements such as feathers around the perimeter. 10. Place the second shape (design side up) on top of glue. Air-dry the fan.
Assessment	• Students verbally identify several self-control choices they have when responding to any volatile situation. • Students role play situations that are likely to result in strong emotions. Can students clearly verbalize feelings? What viable suggestions do they offer for calming down? • Ask students to reflect on this lesson and write a DREAM statement to summarize the most important things they learned.

Extensions		
Younger students or those with physical challenges could decorate just one paper and accordion fold it. Play "Feelings" charades during which students non-verbally act out different emotions written on cards. Practice conflict resolution strategies until children regularly use them.	Attach yarn loops to fans to hang from cubby hooks or chairs for easy access. Encourage students to start an *I Have Self-Control* journal. Suggest that they identify their feelings, the circumstances surrounding them, and how they used self-control in dealing with them.	Formalize a classroom process for dealing with conflicts. Students who are gifted in using conflict resolution strategies role play their skills for younger children. Plan and present a practical program about anger management to families in the school. Use skits, art projects, and other strategies to deliver the message.

Spanish Fans
20th Century
Handpainted wood, silk
Height 8"
Collection of Sandra Lee Wood.

Crayola **Dream~Makers**
Building fun and creativity into standards-based learning

Things Are Not Always as They Appear

Objectives

Students gain respect for creative ideas as they make prints of imaginative happenings or objects and reflect on their classmates' creations.

Students adapt art techniques and approaches based on the Surrealism Movement as they engage in creative thinking.

Multiple Intelligences

Linguistic	Naturalist

National Standards

Visual Arts Standard #1 Understanding and applying media, techniques, and processes **Visual Arts Standard #5** Reflecting upon and assessing the characteristics and merits of their work and the work of others	**Social Studies Standard #1** Culture—experiences that provide for the study of culture and cultural diversity. **Health Education Standard #7** Students will demonstrate the ability to practice health-enhancing behaviors and avoid or reduce health risks.

Background Information

When things do not make sense or when characters, events, and settings are so fantastical that they are not believable, they often are called *surreal*. Artists called Surrealists mixed dream images with their imaginations to express new emotions and to encourage viewers to think deeply about their images. In some cases, Surrealists were saying that dreams are as real as waking thoughts.

The artist Salvador Dali (Spanish, 1904-1989) was considered a leader in the Surrealism Movement in the early 20th century. Throughout his career, he experimented with several styles and different media. One of his famous paintings, called *The Persistence of Memory*, features melting watches. Later in life he turned to images with scientific, historical, and religious themes.

Vocabulary List

Use this list to explore new vocabulary, create idea webs, or brainstorm related subjects.

Absurd
Creativity
Dali
Dream
Fantastical
Imagine/imaginary
Improbable
Magritte
Movement

Open-minded
Press
Print-making
Ridiculous
Surreal/Surrealism/Surrealist

Resources

Dinner at Magritte's by Michael Garland
A storybook for children ages 6 to 9 about what happens when Surrealistic artists come to dine. This fanciful book is told in Magritte-style oil paintings that use many of the artist's favorite symbols.

Imagine That! Activities and Adventures in Surrealism by Joyce Raimondo
For grades 1 to 4. Asks questions about the art of this interesting style. Includes pictures of children's art inspired by Surrealists.

Look-Alikes: Discover a Land Where Things Are Not as They Appear by Joan Steiner
There are limitless visual possibilities! As the tagline says, "The more you look, the more you see" with everyday objects in extraordinary settings.

The King Who Rained by Fred Gwynne
A clever book for all ages, it pokes fun at the complexities of the English language with goofy illustrations.

Artwork by students from Governor Wolf Elementary School, Bethlehem, Pennsylvania.
Teacher: Patricia Check

"Scissors-Man"

Artwork by students from
St. Theresa School,
Hellertown, Pennsylvania.

"Scissors-Man"

What Does It Mean?

Incongruous: odd, illogical, not typical

Movement: suggestion of motion in art

Surrealism: art that units dreams or fantasies with realistic subjects, usually in surprising, incongruous ways

	K-2	3-4	5-6

Suggested Preparation and Discussion

Display the art of surrealist artists such as Salvador Dali and Rene Magritte. Try to identify the incongruous images and events. Why do you think the artist combined them?

Discuss how healthy it is to keep an open mind about others' creative ideas. Creative thinkers generate both novel AND useful ideas, so it is to be celebrated. Creativity stretches original thinking. Ideas and art can strike people as absurd. Imagine living in a house made from mousetraps. What would you think of a card player with plumber's plungers on both cheeks sitting on a chair made of crackers and cheese?

Ask students to think about whether they are timid thinkers who draw back from the incongruous or curious people who prefer a closer look at even the most ridiculous. Talk about what people can learn even in an improbable scenario.

As a class, brainstorm lists or make idea webs of possible topics: people (acquaintances, historic figures, imaginary), places, objects (invented, yet-to-be designed), and actions. Each student then connects at least two contradictory and dissimilar concepts to inspire unusual images.

Crayola® Supplies

- Colored Pencils • Glue Sticks • Markers • Scissors

Other Materials

- Construction paper • Drawing paper • Masking tape
- Recycled foam produce trays • Recycled newspaper
- Spray bottle • White paper

Set-up/Tips

- Cover art surface with recycled newspaper.
- To print letters and numbers correctly, draw them with dark markers on thin white paper. Turn paper over and trace onto foam plate.

The Wisdom of Trees
© 2007 John Thomas
Acrylic on board
24" x 32"
Private Collection.

Untitled
Artist unknown
Painted stoneware
10" x 5" x 4"
Private Collection.

**Process:
Session 1
20-30 min.**

Create printing plate

1. Cut off the edges of clean, foam produce trays to make flat printing plates.
2. Place foam plates on paper. Trace along the outside of the foam plate perimeters with colored pencils.
3. Draw an improbable scene within the outlined space.
4. Tape the drawing to the smooth side of the foam plate. Trace over the drawing with the tip of a pencil. Press hard to make an indentation. Remove the drawing and make sure that all outlines appear on the printing plate.

**Process:
Session 2
15-20 min.**

Print with the plate

5. With markers, cover raised surfaces of printing plates with color.
6. Mist clean drawing paper with sprayer bottles.
7. When paper is damp to touch, place color-coated plate face down on paper. Apply gentle pressure to back of plate.
8. Carefully lift plate off paper to reveal the image. Air-dry the print.
9. Repeat process for more prints or to add colors.

**Process:
Session 3
20-30 min.**

Display and reflect on the prints

10. Attach prints to construction paper for display.
11. View assembled artwork. Try to identify the incongruous images used.

Assessment

- Students follow directions. They can explain the printing process and its use of reverse images.
- Ask children to make two positive comments about each classmate's Surreal scenario.
- Ask students to reflect on this lesson and write a DREAM statement to summarize the most important things they learned.

Extensions

Younger children and some with physical challenges could create their printing plates by drawing directly on the foam plate. Demonstrate the reverse-image process.

Make printing plates or small stamps for alphabet letters and numerals.

Write new words to create "silly songs." Give a surreal concert performance. Design a stage backdrop in the style of a Surrealist artist. Encourage attendees to dress accordingly.

Ask students to look for examples of Surrealism found on video and in print media. Why are they considered surreal?

Try printmaking with other surfaces and designs.

Invite members from the local creative community to speak about where they get their ideas, what feeds their creative juices, and what they do when they have creative blocks.

Suggest that students start dream journals. Use dreams to inspire creative writing, especially poetry.

Make prints using several different plates and paint colors.

Gifted students could learn more about Automatic writing and the Surrealist Movement. Try the technique.

Indonesian Monkey Puppet
Artist Unknown
Ikat fabric, paint, wood
8" x 4" x 6"
Private Collection.

Heroes and Heroines Wanted!

Objectives

Students each identify attributes of one individual who exemplifies the behaviors of a hero or heroine.

Students build low-relief faces for a "Wanted" poster reflecting personality characteristics and responsible actions attributed to their heroes and heroines.

Multiple Intelligences

Interpersonal   Linguistic

National Standards

Visual Arts Standard #2 Using knowledge of structures and functions	**Social Studies Standard #5** Individuals, Groups, and Institutions—experiences that provide for the study of interactions among individuals, groups, and institutions. **Social Studies Standard #10** Civic Ideals and Practices—experiences that provide for the study of the ideas, principles, and practices of citizenship in a democratic republic. **Health Education Standard #8** Students will demonstrate the ability to advocate for personal, family, and community health.

Background Information

Webster's New World Dictionary (3rd College Edition) defines a hero as any person admired for courage and nobility, someone of great inner strength and courage, who often takes on great responsibility for others.

There are many people in the world who are admired by others as heroes and heroines. The astronauts who were space pioneers are considered by many to be world heroes because of the exploration work they accomplished. People who work for charity—like Mother Teresa (1910-1997) who devoted her life to the love and care of very low-income people whom nobody else would look after—are respected as great by many.

Heroines and heroes are people who have personality traits such as kindness and compassion and who build strength and trust in others are often recognized as heroes. Often these people are given awards such as the Nobel Prize for the great work they accomplish.

Resources

Everyday Heroes by Cecile Schoberle
This easy-reading book helps children to see that heroes and their actions happen all around them.

Fifty American Heroes Every Kid Should Meet
by Dennis Denenberg
A compilation of biographies featuring people with a wide variety of backgrounds and ethnicities. Aimed at third to sixth graders, the book includes a quiz to guide further research.

Finding Courage: History's Young Heroes and Their Amazing Deeds by J.M. Bedell
An anthology of stories about young people around the world and throughout history. Inspiring to young people in the middle grades and above.

Vocabulary List

Use this list to explore new vocabulary, create idea webs, or brainstorm related subjects.

Acts	Inner strength
Action	Poster
Bravery	Proportion
Courage	Relief
Emphasis	Responsibility
Hero/Heroine	Texture rubbings
	Valiant
	Wanted

Poster art by 5th grade students,
Alice Carlson Applied Learning Center, Fort Worth, Texas.
Teacher: Elizabeth Harris Willett

What Does It Mean?

Highlight: emphasis that draws attention to part of a work of art

Portrait patterns: repetitive use of shapes when drawing portraits

Proportion: relative size between two or more objects

Texture rubbings: technique in which paper is placed on a rough surface and rubbed with a crayon or other medium

Crayola Dream~Makers

Building fun and creativity into standards-based learning

	K-2	3-4	5-6
Suggested Preparation and Discussion	Discuss questions such as these: What are your responsibilities? What people around you act in responsible ways? One definition of heroism is to take on great responsibility. Who are the heroes and heroines in your life? What heroes and heroines do you know about from the news? What happens when you rub crayon on paper over a raised pattern? Since the pattern is raised, it shows up on the paper above. This texture is called a relief. The process is called crayon rubbings or texture rubbings. Identify heroes and heroines who have made a difference in people's lives. What skills and attributes do they possess?		Brainstorm what kinds of behaviors constitute heroism. Discuss the everyday heroism of police officers or armed forces personnel and the heroism of the moment when action is taken during extraordinary circumstances. Consider: Are the heroes of your early childhood still heroes to you now? Why or why not? Identify heroes and heroines who have made a difference in people's lives. What skills and attributes do they possess?
	Consider color and all the positive symbolic attributes associated with color in creating artwork.		

Crayola® Materials
- Crayons or Oil Pastels
- School Glue
- Scissors

Other Materials
- Construction paper
- Masking tape (optional)
- Oak tag or cardboard
- Recycled cardboard

Set-up/Tips
- Tape sheets together at corners to avoid possible shifting when making rubbings.

Blue is often a color that symbolizes trust, loyalty, wisdom, intelligence, faith, truth, and heaven. Presenting artwork with a blue color theme to someone or giving them a blue crayon can mean you recognize the symbolism attributed to them and the color.

Process: **Session 1** **20-30 min.**	**Create a portrait** 1. Ask students to bring in pictures of their hero/heroine's face. 2. Sketch and cut out a large round or oval head on oak tag. 3. From the leftover edges, cut out simple facial features such as ovals for eyes and a triangle for a nose. 4. Glue features to head. Build up layers of cutouts to form a relief portrait. Add expression and complexity by gluing smaller shapes on top of larger ones. 5. Place the layered portrait on an oak tag base in a position to emphasize its importance. Glue it in place. Air-dry the glue.
Process: **Session 2** **20-30 min.**	**Make a texture rubbing** 6. Place construction paper on top of portrait. 7. Remove wrappers from crayons. Rub the crayon sides over the paper in one direction to reveal portrait patterns. 8. Use additional colors to highlight certain areas of the face.
Process: **Session 3** **20-30 min.**	**Label the poster** 9. Write WANTED across top of poster. Make it large in proportion to the space. 10. Under the portrait, write a slogan or words that feature the heroic behaviors of the person in the portrait.
Assessment	• Students identify worthy attributes of a hero/heroine. • Portraits feature the relief technique. Posters emphasize the hero/heroine's portrait and the WANTED title. • Ask students to reflect on this lesson and write a DREAM statement to summarize the most important things they learned.
Extensions	Ask children if they see themselves as heroes/heroines in the making. What sorts of responsibilities do you practice now? What responsibilities could you take on in your home or classroom? Propose these to a parent or teacher. Honor local heroes and heroines. Invite honorees to attend an awards ceremony, planned by students. Some students with special needs may prefer to cut or tear magazine pictures for their posters. Use assistive technology as necessary to prepare text for the posters. Gifted students could identify heroes and heroines in different fields (health care or human rights, for example), countries, and time periods.	No one can know how one will respond in an emergency. Read true accounts about everyday heroes and heroines. Role play situations that call for heroic action. Identify heroes and heroines in different fields (health care or human rights, for example), countries, and time periods as they arise in the curriculum.

The rubbings seen here were made by rubbing color sticks over bas-relief sculpture from Asia. This rubbing process is similar to the process described in the lesson.

Asian Rubbings
Paper, wax crayon
12" x 26"
Private Collection.

Objectives

Students write compassionate messages to be delivered to individuals who need encouragement.

Students deliver their messages on the wings of paper airplanes that they construct and decorate.

Multiple Intelligences

| Interpersonal | Logical-mathematical |
| Linguistic | |

National Standards

| **Visual Arts Standard #2**
Using knowledge of structures and functions | **Social Studies Standard #5**
Individuals, Groups, and Institutions—experiences that provide for the study of interactions among individuals, groups, and institutions. |
| | **Health Education Standard #4**
Students will demonstrate the ability to use interpersonal communication skills to enhance health and avoid or reduce health risks. |

Background Information

Today, e-mail and instant messaging top the list of speedy ways to communicate, but often these messages are impersonal. Throughout history, many cultures invented unique forms of communication. In the first and second centuries, the Chinese started using paper folding to express themselves.

In 1965, Braniff Airlines commissioned the artist Alexander Calder to refresh the airlines' image. With his creative talents and a DC-8 airplane as his canvas, Calder designed a flying piece of art. The flourish of Calder's signature was visible above the forward cabin door. Images of this plane can be found on the Internet.

Resources

Charlotte's Web by E.B. White
Wonderful illustrations by Garth Williams. Classic tale of compassion across species appeals to young and old alike.

Chicken Soup for the Kid's Soul: 101 Stories of Courage, Hope and Laughter by Jack Canfield
For readers in grades 4 through 6 (younger children enjoy hearing some of the selections). Includes stories submitted by some famous people but mostly by children.

Sam and the Lucky Money by Karen Chinn
Boldly illustrated picture book for preschool through second graders. Chinn tells the compassionate struggle of a young Chinese boy in terms that all children can relate to closely.

Vocabulary List

Use this list to explore new vocabulary, create idea webs, or brainstorm related subjects.

Airplane
Balance
Care/caring
Card
Communicate/communication
Compassion
Deliver
Fly
Fold
Form
Helping
Letter

Line
Kindness
Message
Paper
Pattern
Pilot
Plane
Wings

Artwork by students from
Paxinosa Elementary School,
Easton, Pennsylvania.
Teacher: Cathy Ziegenfuss

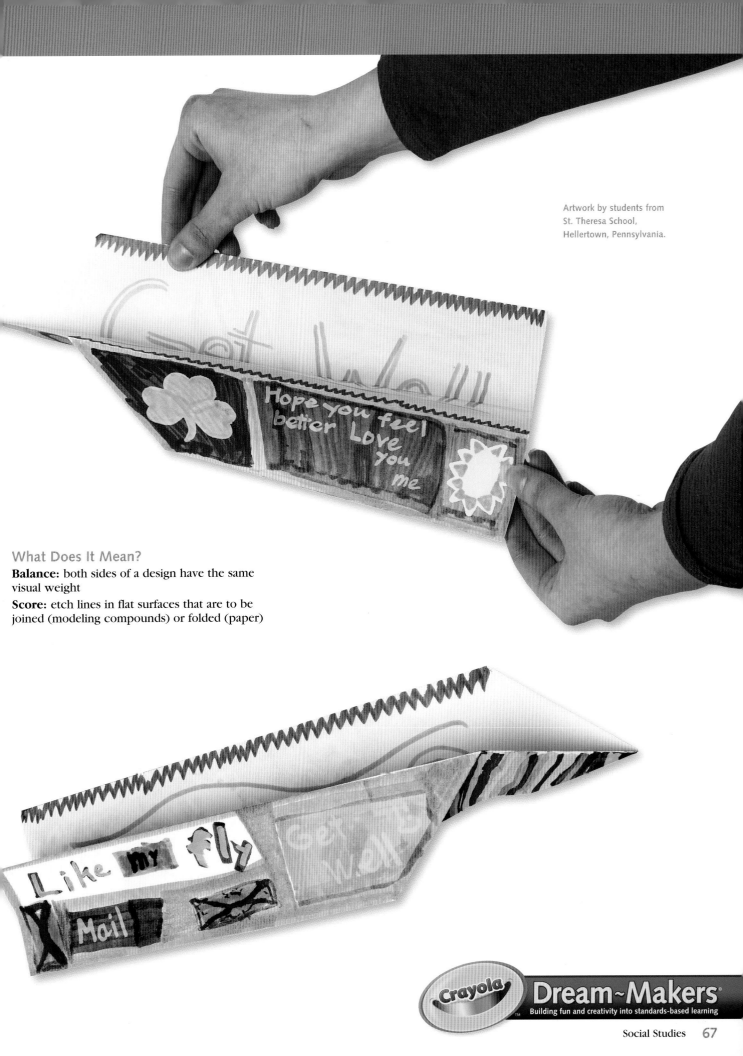

What Does It Mean?

Balance: both sides of a design have the same
visual weight

Score: etch lines in flat surfaces that are to be
joined (modeling compounds) or folded (paper)

	K-2	3-4	5-6
Suggested Preparation and Discussion	Questions to discuss: Can you imagine how a friend might feel who just lost a pet? How do you feel when you see people who are having a difficult time? How could you help them know you care? Identify someone you know who would appreciate a caring message. Perhaps they are sad or lonely. Think about what you could say that would show compassion to them.	Discuss: What are your feelings when you listen to news stories about tragedies? Are you relieved they didn't happen to you? Or are you filled with compassion (the ability to sympathize with another's distress together with a wish to make it better)? Identify someone in your community who would appreciate a caring message. Think about what you could say that would show compassion to them.	
Crayola® Supplies	• Markers		
Other Materials	• White paper		

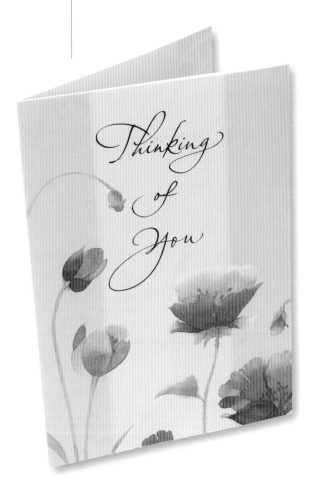

"The Oak Tree"

A Message
Of Encouragement

A mighty wind blew night and day.
It stole the oak tree's leaves away,
Then snapped its boughs
and pulled its bark
until the oak was tired and stark.
But still the oak tree held its ground
while other trees fell all around...

Hallmark Cards

Process:
Session 1
20-30 min.

Make the plane

1. Encourage students to invent their own paper-folding methods. These directions describe how to make the planes pictured. Fold paper in half horizontally and score at fold. Open.

2. Create a triangular point by pulling one upper corner down to center fold and then other corner. Fold together in half.

3. Fold one side down to bottom fold. Fold down other side.

4. Repeat diagram Step 4 for even sleeker plane. Make sure the plane is balanced.

Process:
Session 2
20-30 min.

Write a message

5. Write a caring message on the plane's wings.

6. To decorate the plane, experiment with lines and colors. Fill in areas around message with patterns. Choose an embellishment style that is compatible with the message.

7. Sign and date the flying message. Deliver it personally or slip it into a stamped, addressed envelope and mail it.

Assessment

- Do children exhibit feelings of goodwill and compassion as they write their messages?
- Are messages clearly written on a folded-paper airplane? Is the airplane artfully decorated in a way that is compatible with the message?
- Ask children to report when messages were delivered and how the recipient responded.
- Ask students to reflect on this lesson and write a DREAM statement to summarize the most important things they learned.

Extensions

Read children's literature about individuals whose lives are dedicated to caring for others. Create a display highlighting the compassionate acts of these people.
Experiment with other ways to fold paper airplanes. Which ones fly the highest? Farthest? Straightest?
Experiment with other paper sculpture forms that also carry a compassionate message.
Learn about Sadako and her paper crane project.
Find out about the World Peace Project for Children.
Seek ways to exhibit compassion within your community and beyond. Choose projects suitable for children's ages.
Adapt paper-folding techniques as applicable for children with special needs.
Gifted children could write more extensive messages on more elaborately folded airplanes.

How to fold a paper plane

Step 1. Lay paper lengthwise.

Step 2. Fold paper in half.

FOLD

Step 3. Fold corners back on both sides.

FOLD

Step 4. Fold top edge down to center fold on both sides.

FOLD

Step 5. Folding is complete.

Crayola **Dream~Makers**
Building fun and creativity into standards-based learning

Mindful Masks

Objectives

Students recognize the cultural uses of masks and identify a strong feeling or emotion to represent in their own masks.

Students create masks that focus on color, texture, and pattern to reflect the emotions of a particular situation, and reflect on how each others' work communicates that emotion.

Multiple Intelligences

Bodily-kinesthetic
Intrapersonal

What Does It Mean?

Mottled: blotches of color or texture

Art principles: use of art elements to achieve balance, repetition/rhythm/pattern, unity, contrast, variety, proportion, emphasis, and movement in a work of art

National Standards

Visual Arts Standard #3
Changing and evaluating a range of subject matter, symbols, and ideas

Visual Arts Standard #5
Reflecting upon and assessing the characteristics and merits of their work and the work of others

Social Studies Standard #1
Culture—experiences that provide for the study of culture and cultural diversity.

Health Education Standard #4
Students will demonstrate the ability to use interpersonal communication skills to enhance health and avoid or reduce health risks.

Background Information

People have worn masks since ancient times as both functional and beautiful objects. They are used to ward off evil spirits, provide self-defense, celebrate holidays and commemorations, and transform the wearer into something different than self.

Early cave paintings in Lascaux, France (ca. 15000 BCE) depict hunters wearing masks that resemble the animals they hunted. Ancient Egyptians in the second century AD made portrait masks of their dead. Details of the face were painted around glass eyes that were fitted on the mask. In Bali, Hindu dancers wear different masks to portray the powers of good and evil during the epic dance of Ramayana. Some tribes in Africa and Alaska wear masks when performing hunting rituals today. During Mardi Gras celebrations around the world, people wear masks to free themselves from who and what they are the rest of the year.

Resources

How Are You Peeling? by Saxton Freymann
A joy for all ages, the author transforms real fruits and vegetables into people's many moods with rhyming text.

Making Masks by Renee Schwarz
A how-to book for 9- to 12-year-olds. Clear, step-by-step instructions for 13 creative masks.

The Amazing Book of Shapes by Lydia Sharman
A book with a lot of eye appeal. It encourages independent exploration of the topic for second to sixth graders.

Vocabulary List

Use this list to explore new vocabulary, create idea webs, or brainstorm related subjects.

Communication
Disguise
Emotion
Express
Expression
Face
Feeling
Hide
Mask
Masquerade
Mood
Pattern

Revel
Ritual
Sentiment
Texture
Transform
Veil

Mexican Festival Mask
1991
Artist: Juan Horta
Painted wood
Height 12 1/2"
Tocuaro, Michoacan, Mexico
Private Collection.

Artwork by students from Weisenberg Elementary School, Kutztown, Pennsylvania.
Teacher: R. De Long

Indonesian Face Mask
20th Century
Painted wood
Height 8 1/2"
Private Collection.

Malaysian Face Mask
20th Century
Painted wood
Height 12"
Private Collection.

Crayola Dream~Makers®
Building fun and creativity into standards-based learning

Mindful Masks

	K-2	3-4	5-6
Suggested Preparation and Discussion	Ask children to discuss how they can tell what someone might be feeling about a situation: by looks on their faces, their body posture, or what they say, for example. What facial expressions often reveal strong emotions? How could those feelings be expressed in a mask through shape, color, pattern, and texture?	Discuss how people in various cultures and during special times wear masks to temporarily transform themselves into new roles. How do facial features on masks express, or disguise, emotions of the wearer? Together, figure out how art elements and principles such as shape, color, pattern, and texture can express emotional ideas.	How is emotion portrayed visually? Discuss examples. Analyze masks from several cultures, based on their function and time period. In that culture, what colors appear to express happiness? Which textures might portray nervousness or shyness? What colors or patterns could convey hurt? Brainstorm ideas about how art elements and principles such as shape, color, pattern, and texture can express emotional ideas.

Display examples of masks and pictures of masks from different parts of the world, various time periods, and those used for a range of purposes. Discuss materials used to make them.

Children each choose a situation in which a feeling can be portrayed in a unique mask.

Crayola® Supplies

• Colored Pencils • Markers • Paint Brushes • School Glue • Scissors • Tempera Paint (white)

Other Materials

• Masking tape • Oak tag or recycled file folders • Paper towels • Recycled newspapers
• Scrap papers to shred • Water containers • White paper

Set-up/Tips

• Ask parent volunteers to shred paper beforehand.
• Cover painting surface with recycled newspaper.
• Dilute paint with an equal amount of water.
• Instead of a paper tube, a tree branch, craft stick, or dowel stick can also be used for a handle.

Artwork by students from Weisenberg Elementary School, Kutztown, Pennsylvania.
Teacher: R. De Long

Process: Session 1 20-30 min.	**Make mask form** 1. Cut out a large mask in a shape that can help convey the chosen emotion. Write the emotion to be portrayed on the back of mask. 2. Hold mask to face. An adult lightly marks places for eyes, noses, and mouths with colored pencils. 3. Cut out facial features.
Process: Session 2 15-20 min.	**Decorate mask** 4. Experiment with markers to use line, color, pattern, and texture to express the mask's emotion. 5. Lightly brush diluted white paint across the entire design to create a pastel effect. 6. Blot the surface with paper towels for a mottled look. Air-dry the paint. 7. Redraw any design elements that are too subdued.
Process: Session 3 20-30 min.	**Assemble mask** 8. Glue shredded paper strips or other shapes around the mask's perimeter. Air-dry the glue. 9. Tightly roll a paper tube for the handle. Glue the open edge. Glue handle to back of mask. Air-dry glue.
Assessment	• Students present their masks to classmates to identify the emotion. • Children reflect on how they used art techniques to express emotion. • Ask students to reflect on this lesson and write a DREAM statement to summarize the most important things they learned.
Extensions	Younger students and children with special needs may make a large oval mask, which is easier to cut out. Decorate the surrounding area. Role-play problem-solving situations in which the strong emotions chosen are central. What actions can students take to either celebrate or constructively handle those strong emotions?	Conduct mime sessions in which students act out emotions wordlessly for others to identify. Students each choose a cultural or historic mask for in-depth research. Write reports and present findings to classmates. Suggest that students identify times when they have strong emotions. Ask them to record words that describe those feelings.	How do different cultures portray emotions? Study masks used to tell stories or for various celebrations and events. Gifted students could write a play using masks to convey meaning. Study Kabuki Theatre and its use of masks.

How to make a whole mask

Step 1. Adult marks areas with simple shapes on paper where facial features should appear.

Step 2. Students gently fold paper over area where shapes appear and snip away a small triangular shape. They insert scissors and cut out shape. Use Crayola Cutter™ if available.

Step 3. Cut away outside edges to create a face shape. Punch holes to attach ribbon or string.

How to make a half mask

Step 1. Have adult mark where eye spaces are located.

Step 2. Cut out eye and nose shapes.

Step 3. Punch holes on sides of mask. Attach ribbon or yarn to holes for ties.

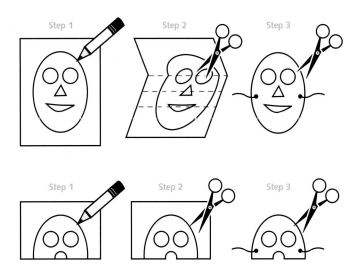

"Reigning Respect" Crowns

Objectives

Students identify behaviors that inspire people's respect and that demonstrate their respect to others.

Students use graphic symbols, words, and patterns to design a crown intended to encourage respectful behavior.

Multiple Intelligences

Interpersonal
Intrapersonal
Linguistic

What Does It Mean?

Symbol: image that represents an idea or object

Motto: theme or slogan

National Standards

Visual Arts Standard #3 Choosing and evaluating a range of subject matter, symbols, and ideas	**Social Studies Standard #5** Individuals, Groups, and Institutions—experiences that provide for the study of individual development and identity.
	Health Education Standard #2 Students will analyze the influence of family, peers, culture, media, technology and other factors on health behaviors.
	Health Education Standard #4 Students will demonstrate the ability to use interpersonal communication skills to enhance health and avoid or reduce health risks.

Background Information

Headwear is often practical, protecting the wearer from rain, cold, wind, or snow. Headwear in some cultural traditions also indicates the status and achievements of the wearer. In Uganda, the word *head* means elder and signifies a person with great wisdom, experience, and moral influence. Among the Tuareg people of Africa, men wear turbans and face veils every day. Throughout the day, they change the position of the veil and turban to indicate to others their importance and need to be respected.

Resources

Crowing Achievements: African Arts of Dressing the Head
by Mary Jo Arnoldi and Christine Kreamer
Scholarly reference book filled with photographs.
Complied by two Smithsonian curators.

Hats, Hats, Hats by Ann Morris
Colorful, ethnically diverse photographs of headgear. Includes detailed background about each hat's origin.

Respect by Lucia Raatma
A starting place to explore the topic with elementary school children.

Vocabulary List

Use this list to explore new vocabulary, create idea webs, or brainstorm related subjects.

Character	Leader
Crown	Pattern
Earn	Respect
Hat	Shape
Head	
Headdress	
Headgear	
Headwear	
Lead	

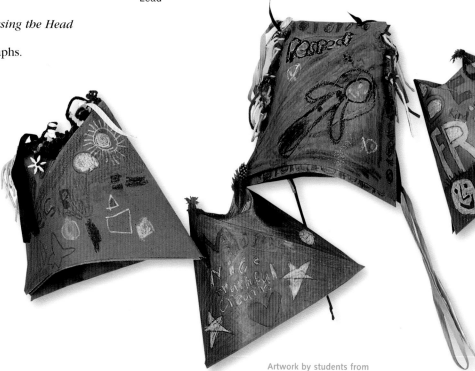

Artwork by students from
Freemansburg Elementary School,
Freemansburg, Pennsylvania.
Teacher: Barbara Kozero

Artwork by students from
St. Theresa School,
Hellertown, Pennsylvania.

"Reigning Respect" Crowns

	K-2	3-4	5-6
Suggested Preparation and Discussion	Brainstorm about what kinds of behaviors inspire people to respect each other. How do students show their respect? What words describe the character quality known as respect?		
	Discuss people students know who wear things on their heads and why. Read stories about crown-wearing royalty. What messages do crowns convey to others?	Examine pictures of different types of headgear from groups of people around the world. What colors and symbols in various cultures represent respect?	Talk about what students wear on their heads and why, such as team alliances, religious tradition, or fashion statements. How can respect be visually portrayed without words? Use of color, line, shape, and pattern?
Crayola® Supplies	• Construction Paper™ Crayons • Glitter Glue • School Glue • Scissors		
Other Materials	• Brown paper bags • Chenille stems • Craft paper • Decorative craft materials • Hole punch • Paper towels • Ribbon or yarn		
Set-up/Tips	• Ask a grocery store to donate enough paper bags for the class. • Paper squares need to be large enough to cover head when folded—about 20 inches (51 cm).		

Felt jester hat
Artist unknown
Private Collection.

Hats worn by Asian children reflect history, culture, and family.

Indian chief headdress, regalia, and vest. Headdresses were a symbol of pride, prestige, and honor in a tribe.

Process:
Session 1
20-30 min.

Shape the crown

1. Cut paper bags into 20-inch or larger squares.
2. With the fold at the bottom, fold point A so the point touches point AA on the right diagonal edge. Fold in half, point to point. Crease hard.
3. Bring the bottom point B of triangle across to opposite edge point BB.
4. Push one layer of top point of triangle down into pocket. Crease. Press second flap into the hat.
5. Turn hat shape over and repeat diagram on other side.

Process:
Session 2
15-20 min.

Decorate the crown

6. Draw symbols and words that reflect respected behavior on both sides with crayons and oil pastels.
7. Fill the space surrounding the signs of respect with patterns, borders, and designs.
8. For a shiny effect, rub crayon-covered designs or areas with bits of paper towel.

Process:
Session 3
20-30 min.

Embellish crown

9. Glue on plastic jewels, feathers, and other embellishments.
10. Punch holes along edges. Tie chenille stems, yarn, and ribbon pieces to top and sides. Add Glitter Glue. Air-dry the glitter glue.

Assessment

• Respectful behaviors are clearly illustrated and written on crowns.	• Symbols, designs, and words used on crowns convey a sense of respect.

- Crowns are constructed according to directions. They are decorated in original, unique ways using art elements such as pattern and color.
- Ask students to reflect on this lesson and write a DREAM statement to summarize the most important things they learned.

Extensions

Display crowns in classroom to remind students of appropriate behavior.

Devise, with students' help, a system to promote respectful behavior.

Role play situations in which children practice respectful behaviors, even when it is difficult to do so.

Students with some physical challenges may need assistance to fold their crowns.

Bestow respect crowns on each other to acknowledge admirable behavior.

Conduct a school-wide effort to generate respect slogans. Vote to adopt one as the school motto.

Read children's literature that models respectful behavior. Turn scenes into skits to demonstrate these behaviors to younger children.

Sculpt people in history or within the community who have earned respect. Display crowns on these figures.

Gifted students research other cultures and time periods to learn more about headgear and its meaning. Prepare a presentation with original art based on the various types of head coverings.

How to fold a hat

Step 1

Step 2

Step 3

Step 4

A   AA   BB   B

Step 5

Bottom of hat

Top of hat

Scepters for Benevolent Leaders

Objectives

Students research information about symbols of leadership in various cultures and time periods and identify benevolent leaders.

Students create decorative scepters crowned with three-dimensional symbols of group membership for presentation to the person identified as a benevolent leader.

Multiple Intelligences

Interpersonal

Spatial

What Does It Mean?

Benevolent: kind and generous to others without expecting anything in return

Blend: in the case of blending mix two or more colors or media

Scepter: wand used as a symbol of political power

Topper: 3-D form attached to the highest point

National Standards

Visual Arts Standard #4 Understanding the visual arts in relation to history and cultures	**Social Studies Standard #1** Culture—experiences that provide for the study of culture and cultural diversity. **Social Studies Standard #6** Power, Authority, and Governance—experiences that provide for the study of how people create and change structures of power, authority, and governance.
	Health Education Standard #2 Students will analyze the influence of family, peers, culture, media, technology, and other factors on health behaviors.

Background Information

Signs and symbols are historic and found in all cultures. Some symbols are recognizable, such as the alphabet. Others, of uncertain and ancient origin, may mean different things to different people. These symbols have enriched people's understanding about their cultures, expressed feelings about leaders, and even revealed fears.

Scepters are staffs carried by leaders and rulers as emblems of their governing authority. Throughout history, crafters who designed royal scepters incorporated symbols of animals, objects, people, places, and actions. These symbols reflect complex ideas and traditions. During the Middle Ages, kingly power came to be symbolized by a scepter carried in the right hand. A second staff known as the "Hand of Justice" was carried in the left, with a hand in the act of blessing atop it.

Resources

100 Things You Should Know About Kings and Queens
by Fiona MacDonald
Children's humor and imagination are sprinkled through this accessible historical survey book.

Asante Kingdom by Carol Thompson
Written by an African art expert. Displays and explains real objects of an important African tribe, the Asante, for elementary students.

Dictionary of Symbolism: Cultural Icons and the Meanings Behind Them by Hans Biedermann
A to Z guide to more than 2,000 symbols and their meanings. Definite fodder for a middle school student's visual vocabulary.

Quiltmaker's Gift by Jeff Brumbeau
Beautifully illustrated picture book about a king who changes from greedy to benevolent leader. Told with moving warmth and applies to all ages.

Vocabulary List

Use this list to explore new vocabulary, create idea webs, or brainstorm related subjects.

Balance
Benevolence/benevolent
Cane
Ceremonial
Crown
Fair
Form
Good
Govern
Just
King
Lead
Leader
Line
Object
Pattern
Queen
Royal
Royalty
Rule
Ruler
Scepter
Sculpt
Shapes
Sign

Staff
Symbol
Texture
Throne
Unity

Top of religious scepter
Artist unknown
Private Collection.

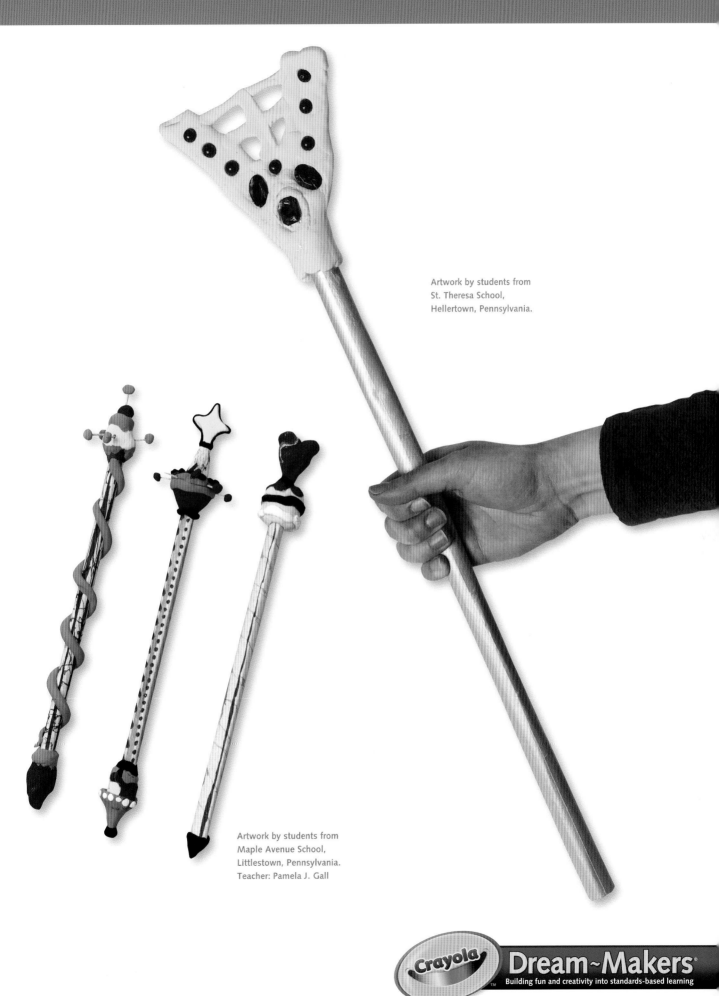

Artwork by students from
St. Theresa School,
Hellertown, Pennsylvania.

Artwork by students from
Maple Avenue School,
Littlestown, Pennsylvania.
Teacher: Pamela J. Gall

Scepters for Benevolent Leaders

	K-2	3-4	5-6
Suggested Preparation and Discussion	Research and discuss what scepters are and what they symbolize. Point out that scepters are often passed from one leader to another. Brainstorm cartoon characters that hold scepters. Display close-up photographs of scepters from all around world, including ancient Egyptian, Asante, and Medieval Europe scepters. Identify 3-dimensional symbols on the tops and how they are related to the country or leader. Discuss how kind leaders act. *Benevolent* means one who does generous acts for others without expecting anything in return. Think of examples of such leaders from books, movies, and real life. Choose one person to honor symbolically with an original scepter. Review three parts of the scepter that each child will design—staff, symbolic topper, and bottom balance. Discuss how color carries symbolic meaning, such as school colors. Share how simple forms can represent group or individual qualities, such as a tree for an ecology group or a sun for a person with a sunny disposition.		
Crayola® Supplies	• Markers • Model Magic® • School Glue		
Other Materials	• Collage materials such as buttons, craft feathers, toothpicks • Rubber bands • White paper		

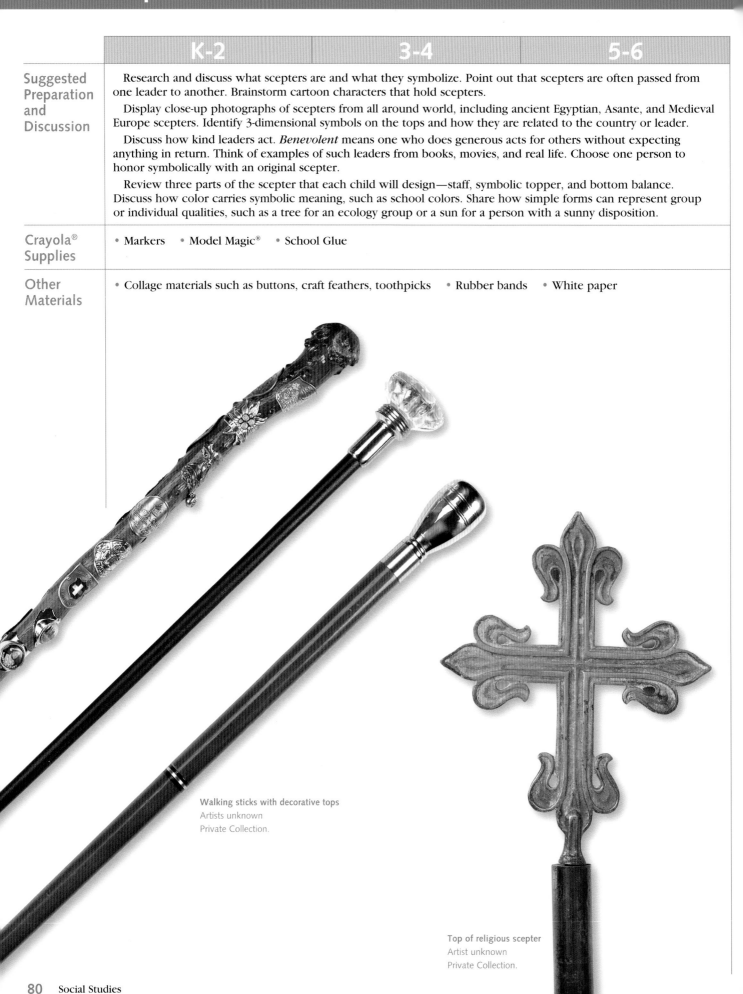

Walking sticks with decorative tops
Artists unknown
Private Collection.

Top of religious scepter
Artist unknown
Private Collection.

Process: Session 1 20-30 min.	**Roll scepter** 1. Place paper on flat surface. From the longer side, roll into a tight tube. Secure with rubber bands. 2. Apply glue along the edge and press. Move bands until all edges are secure. Air-dry the glue.

Process:
Session 2
20-30 min.
	Shape topper and bottom bases
	3. Shape Model Magic compound around one end of tube as the base for the topper symbol.
	4. Form a smaller shape around the bottom of the scepter.
	5. Experiment with mixing and blending Model Magic compound colors using techniques like these:
	  • Blend two primary colors together completely to make a secondary hue.
	  • Add white to colored compound to create tints.
	  • Add black to make shaded tones.
	  • Create marbled effects by partially blending various colors.
	  • Add washable marker color to make new hues.

Process: Session 3 20-30 min.	**Design decorative topper and staff** 6. Model symbols and press these forms firmly onto the base attached to staff. Secure with glue if necessary. 7. Add decoration and texture using collage materials. Strive to achieve a unified look. Air-dry the Model Magic compound. 8. Enhance the surface of the rolled tube with assorted marker shapes, lines, and patterns. 9. Make "presentations" to the benevolent leader, explaining to the class why that person is being honored.
Assessment	• Children's scepters accurately portray the qualities of the benevolent leader they identified. • Children symbolically bestow their scepters to a person who is a benevolent leader and explain why that person was chosen for the honor. • Children can identify the meanings of each other's scepter toppers. • Ask students to reflect on this lesson and write a DREAM statement to summarize the most important things they learned.
Extensions	Discuss how one feels when one does something for another person. Share examples of benevolent behavior. Compile a class book with photos of the scepters and descriptions of why recipients were chosen for the honor. Students with special needs might identify someone they know personally for the honor. Provide assistance as needed to help identify the person and determine the characteristics of benevolence that they exhibit. Record benevolent acts observed in school on a chart.	Is there anything that acts as a scepter for today's leaders? Would it help leaders to have a physical manifestation of their power and responsibility? Why? Design a monthly "benevolence" award for student and faculty nominated by individuals or groups. Gifted students could write a play, develop authentic period costumes, and award their scepters accordingly.

Gifts From the Heart

Objectives

Students identify an organization or facility to be the recipient of their gift mural and identify an appropriate theme for the mural's message.

Students paint a large-scale, meaningful, unified assemblage to be presented as a gift.

Multiple Intelligences

Bodily-kinesthetic	Spatial
Interpersonal	

National Standards

Visual Arts Standard #3 Choosing and evaluating a range of subject matter, symbols, and ideas	**Social Studies Standard #3** People, Places, and Environments—experiences that provide for the study of people, place, and environments.
	Health Education Standard #4 Students will demonstrate the ability to use interpersonal communication skills to enhance health and avoid or reduce health risks.

Background Information

In 1482, artist and inventor Leonardo daVinci was commissioned to sculpt a life-size horse. The sculpture called "il Cavallo" was to be a symbol of power and grace for its patron, Duke Ludovico Sforza of Milan, Italy. War prevented daVinci from completing the statue.

More than 500 years later, a Pennsylvanian, Charles Dent began a similar statue, which he never completed either. Nina Akamu finished "il Cavallo" after Dent's death. With the hard work of many people the Akamu "il Cavallo" was presented to Milan as a gift from the people of the United States.

Resources

How to Draw Animals by Jack Hamm
How-to book includes basic and more advanced drawing instruction. Animals are divided by families.

Murals: Walls That Sing by George Ancona
Photo essay that appeals to students up to eighth grade. Includes the philosophy behind this community art form as well as brief background information.

The New Alphabet of Animals by Christopher Wormell
Bold block prints illustrate both exotic and the ordinary animals with washes of color for young children.

Vocabulary List

Use this list to explore new vocabulary, create idea webs, or brainstorm related subjects.

Art
Assemblage
Background
Characteristics
Community
Gift
Heart
Mural
Organization
Paint/painting

Portrait
Proportion
Recipient
Scale
Teamwork
Traits
Unity
Wall

24' Bronze Horse on-site in San Siro
Cultural Park, Milan, Italy
Courtesy Leonardo da Vinci's Horse, Inc.,
P.O. Box 396, Fogelsville, PA 18051-0396
www.leonardoshorse.org

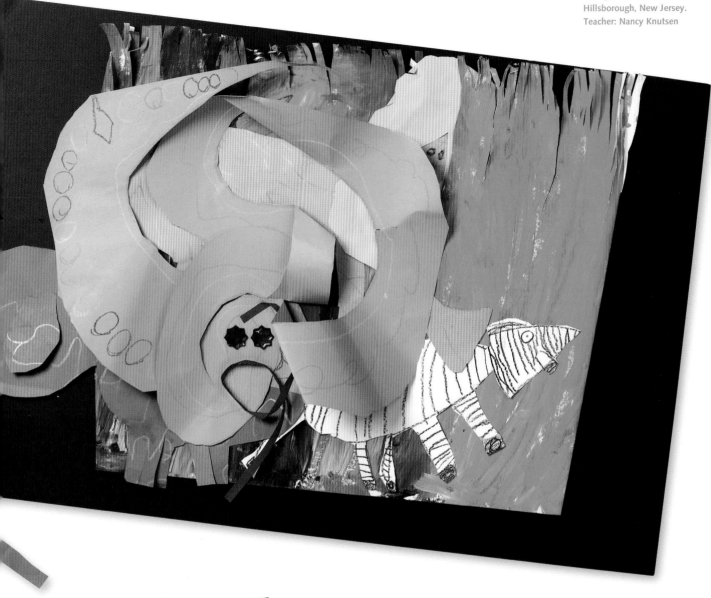

Artwork by students from
Triangle Elementary School,
Hillsborough, New Jersey.
Teacher: Nancy Knutsen

Artwork by students from Alice Carlson
Applied Learning Center,
Fort Worth, Texas.
Teacher: Elizabeth Harris Willett

What Does It Mean?

Assemblage: unified sculpture that combines unrelated objects

Primary hues: the colors red, yellow, and blue.

Secondary hues: the colors orange, green, and violet, created by mixing two primary colors

Crayola **Dream~Makers®**
Building fun and creativity into standards-based learning

	K-2	3-4	5-6
Suggested Preparation and Discussion	Discuss: Have you ever given people gifts that they really loved? How did their appreciation of your gifts make you feel? Sometimes gifts from the heart are given from one group of people to another. What group gifts can you think of? As a class, think about creating a mural, a gift from your heart, to give to another group. Discuss what group would be a deserving recipient. Consider children's hospitals, senior centers and nursing homes, or an animal shelter. Research a suitable theme for the mural. For example, for an animal shelter, if animals are chosen, look at how creatures are depicted in art and in photographs. Discover their distinctive body parts and proportions. Think about what qualities are associated with specific animals and which ones the class wants to be reflected in the mural. Examine Edward Hick's painting "Peaceable Kingdom." Agree upon the mural theme and images that will suitably convey the recipient's message to the public.		
Crayola® Supplies	• Crayons • Paint Brushes • School Glue • Tempera Paint • Scissors		
Other Materials	• Construction paper • Craft paper on a roll • Paper plates • Paper towels • Recycled newspaper • Water containers • Yardstick		
Set-up/Tips	• Cover painting area with newspaper. • On paper plates, mix two primary paint colors together to make secondary hues. • Add white paint to create tints and black to make shades.		

South African Giraffe
Artist unknown
Raku fired and glazed clay
13" x 3" x 7 1/2"
Private Collection.

African Elephant
Artist unknown
Rosewood, ivory
12" x 13" x 8"
Private Collection.

	K-2	3-4	5-6

Process: Session 1 20-30 min.	**Create portraits** 1. Sketch large portraits or other images that suit the mural theme on construction paper. 2. Experiment with drawing and crayon coloring techniques to create hair and other details. Complete the images. 3. Cut out portraits.
Process: Session 2 20-30 min.	**Design the mural** 4. Using a yardstick, draw a border around craft paper. 5. Paint the mural background inside the border. Air-dry the paint.
Process: Session 3 20-30 min.	6. Glue portraits to mural background. Air-dry the glue. 7. Sign first names around border along with warm wishes for the mural's beneficiary. 8. Paint over the portraits and border with diluted paint for a crayon-resist effect. Air-dry the paint. 9. Work together to plan an event in which the mural is presented.
Assessment	• Students work cooperatively to select a theme and design their unified mural. • Students can explain why the mural is suitable as a gift for the recipient. • Students plan and carry out an appropriate recipient presentation. • Ask students to reflect on this lesson and write a DREAM statement to summarize the most important things they learned.
Extensions	Compile an alphabet book of animals or other portraits used on the mural. Draw life-size murals outdoors with Crayola Sidewalk Chalk or Sidewalk Paint. Support children with disabilities by offering assistive technology to facilitate cutting, drawing, and painting.	Gifted students work in small groups to design murals to present information for reports on geographic features, plant growth, or any other topic. Research famous murals, including community mural projects like the one in Philadelphia. Which artists are known for their murals? Why? Consider creating handmade gifts for other occasions.

Charles Dent with clay model
Courtesy Leonardo da Vinci's Horse, Inc.,
P.O. Box 396, Fogelsville, PA 18051-0396
www.leonardoshorse.org

Crayola **Dream~Makers**
Building fun and creativity into standards-based learning

Objectives

Students write encouraging messages to promote honest, trustworthy, and truthful behaviors in others.

Students apply patterns and color to pretend fortune cookie sculptures to contain their thought-provoking messages.

Multiple Intelligences

| Interpersonal | Linguistic |
| Intrapersonal | |

National Standards	
Visual Arts Standard #5 Reflecting upon and assessing the characteristics and merits of their work and work of others	**Social Studies Standard #5** Individuals, Groups, and Institutions—experiences that provide for the study of interactions among individuals, groups, and institutions.
	Health Education Standard #1 Students will comprehend concepts related to health promotion and disease prevention to enhance health.

Background Information

The origin of the fortune cookie is a hotly debated topic. The Chinese have a long tradition of placing messages inside sweets for special occasions such as birth announcements or festival celebrations. The fortune cookie that is common today, however, is an American invention. It might stem from the time when Chinese immigrants were working to build the railroad and could not afford fancier treats. Or the tradition may have started in the early twentieth century when a Chinese baker is said to have handed them out to homeless people with words of encouragement.

Resources

Fortune Cookie Fortunes by Grace Lin
A delightful picture book for kindergarteners through third graders. Fortune cookie messages aptly apply to family members in the story, illustrated in watercolor and origami.

Passport on a Plate: A Round-the-World Cookbook for Children by Diane Simone Vezza and Susan Greenstein
For cooks from fourth to sixth grades. More than 100 worldwide recipes are rated for difficulty.

Vocabulary List

Use this list to explore new vocabulary, create idea webs, or brainstorm related subjects.

Affirmation
Chance
Character
Cheating
China/Chinese
Cookie
Empower
Encourage
Food
Fortune
Honest/honesty

Inspire
Luck
Lying
Message
Pattern
Sculpt
Stealing
Trustworthiness
Truthfulness

Silk Fortune Container
Artist unknown
Silk, cardboard, and thread
2 1/2" x 2"
Private Collection.

Japanese bad fortunes tied to a roadside shrub
Photo by R. De Long

What Does It Mean?

Pattern: orderly, repeated designs

Sculpt: form, carve, and add texture to modeling compound

Symbol: image that represents an idea or object

Japanese fortune bunch
Photo by R. De Long

Artwork by students from
Freemansburg Elementary School,
Freemansburg, Pennsylvania.
Teacher: Patricia Check

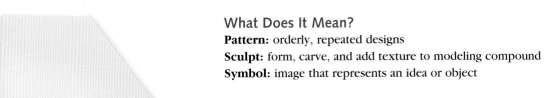

	K-2	3-4	5-6
Suggested Preparation and Discussion	Discuss the virtues of honesty, trustworthiness, and truthfulness. Why are these character traits so valuable in life? Read biographies and stories about the value of honesty. What kind of fortune messages might encourage others to behave honestly? Brainstorm ideas and messages for fortunes that could help others avoid lying, cheating, and stealing. Share a snack of fortune cookies. Talk about their messages and meanings.		
Crayola® Supplies	• Colored Pencils • Markers • Model Magic® • Scissors		
Other Materials	• Modeling tools such as plastic dinner knives, craft sticks, and toothpicks • Waxed paper (optional) • White paper		
Set-up/Tips	• Air-dry folded fortune replicas on waxed paper for at least 24 hours before decorating.		

Tibetan Fortunes
Artists unknown
Red ink on rice paper
2 3/4" x 7"
Private Collection.

Great fortune in business

Progress in studies

Eradicate sickness

Helps maintain and nurture relationships

Peaceful and safe home

Silk Fortune Container
Artist unknown
Silk, cardboard, and thread
2 1/2" x 2"
Private Collection.

K-2	3-4	5-6

Process: Session 1
20-30 min.

Write fortunes

1. Cut several paper strips on which to write honesty-encouraging fortunes.
2. Print simple messages to inspire honesty on the strips with colored pencils.
3. Decorate back and front side of the message with eye-catching marker lines, patterns, and designs.

Process: Session 2
20-30 min.

Create fortune containers

4. Flatten a small Model Magic ball with hands or use a capped marker as rolling pin. Cut into a circle.
5. Place paper fortune across the center of circle. Fold the circle loosely in half. Do not apply pressure.
6. Pull pointed ends of fold together while pushing center out. Pinch edges closed. Air-dry at least 24 hours.

Process: Session 3
20-30 min.

Decorate fortune containers

7. Consider using symbols that offer design clues about the message contained inside.
8. Add marker patterns to outside of "cookies."

Assessment

• Does the message reflect integrity and apply to the theme of honesty?
• How closely does the artistic expression relate to the topic?
• Ask students to reflect on this lesson and write a DREAM statement to summarize the most important things they learned.

Extensions

Try making edible cookies with the help of someone for whom fortune cookies are a family tradition.

Students with some types of motor challenges could print their messages from a computer and make paper envelopes in which to put them.

Find out about other traditional Chinese foods. Compile a book of healthy recipes.

Read children's books that portray situations in which characters confront the issue of dishonesty. Talk about what children can do when they encounter others who do not tell the truth.

Debate: Is honesty always the best policy? What about the lie of omission?

Gifted students could find out about other fortune-telling traditions from around the world. Prepare reports on the most interesting ones, including adages from various cultures about honesty.

Role play situations in which students face everyday challenges to be honest. Discuss which decisions are most honorable. Consider the long-term effects of honesty.

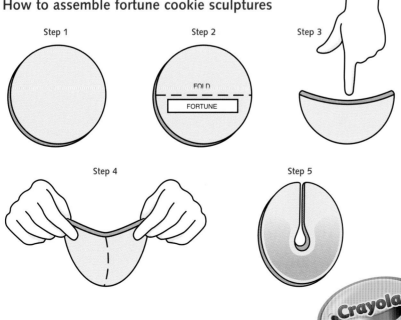

How to assemble fortune cookie sculptures

Step 1

Step 2
FOLD
FORTUNE

Step 3

Step 4

Step 5

Crayola Dream~Makers®
Building fun and creativity into standards-based learning

What's in a Name? Alternatives to Name-Calling!

Objectives

Students identify strategies to respond to and reduce the incidence of name-calling, bullying, and similar hurtful behaviors.

Students use illuminated-manuscript decorative techniques from the Middle Ages to create pages for an illuminated class book that contains constructive choices for reacting to name-calling.

Multiple Intelligences

Interpersonal | Linguistic

National Standards

Visual Arts Standard #5 Reflecting upon and assessing the characteristics and merits of their work and the work of others	**Social Studies Standard #10** Civic Ideals and Practices—experiences that provide for the study of the ideas, principles, and practices of citizenship in a democratic republic.
	Health Education Standard #5 Students will demonstrate the ability to use decision-making skills to enhance health.

Background Information

Before the invention of the printing press (1440), books were hand copied. Called *manuscripts*, each individual page was referred to as a *leaf*. Each leaf often contained highly decorative lettering and borders, sometimes painted with a thin layer of gold or silver (a decorative technique also called leaf).

During the Middle Ages (approximately 440 to 1500) manuscript making was considered a high art. Monks spent hours creating these documents. The monks, or illuminators decorated their writings with very fancy letters that sometimes included animals, landscape images and people. In some of the manuscripts the monks decorated the word columns by surrounding the writing with botanical decoration, or the margins were filled with playful birds, animals, or imaginary beings.

Vocabulary List

Use this list to explore new vocabulary, create idea webs, or brainstorm related subjects.

Bind/binding
Book
Border
Bully/bullying
Decorative
Embellish
Front matter
Hurt
Hurtful
Illumination
Leaf (two meanings)
Manuscript
Mean

Medieval
Middle Ages
Name-calling
Names
Page
Pattern
Shape
Table of contents
Taunts
Tease
Unify
Words

Resources

How to Handle Bullies, Teasers, and Other Meanies: A Book That Takes the Nuisance Out of Name Calling and Other Nonsense by Kate Cohen-Posey
Practical guide for grades 4 through 6, filled with tips. Book's main approach to name-calling is to diffuse with humor (not a solution for everyone).

Illuminations by Jonathan Hunt
ABC format illustrates the technique of illumination as well as provides information about the Middle Ages. Geared to grades 1 through 3.

Words Are Not for Hurting by Elizabeth Verdick
Child-friendly picture book for up to second grade. Discusses the power of words as well as each child's personal responsibility for using that power.

Artwork by students from
Alice Carlson Applied Learning Center,
Fort Worth, Texas.
Teacher: Elizabeth Harris Willett

What Does It Mean?

Embellish: add detail

Illuminate: make resplendent by decorating letters, pages, paragraphs, or borders with colors and gold or silver as was done in the Middle Ages

Leaf: both sides of one page of a book, or covering a surface with a thin layer of gold or silver

Technique: style, skills, and manner of creating art

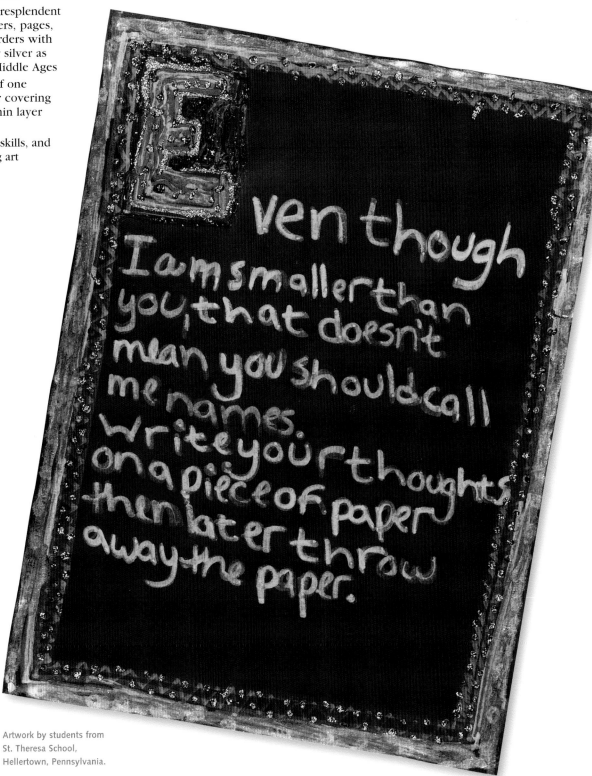

Even though I am smaller than you, that doesn't mean you should call me names. Write your thoughts on a piece of paper then later throw away the paper.

Artwork by students from
St. Theresa School,
Hellertown, Pennsylvania.

	K-2	3-4	5-6
Suggested Preparation and Discussion	Discuss how words are powerful tools to do good in the world as well as to do harm. Words can encourage people to participate in positive behaviors. Talk about examples from students' lives as well as from history and children's literature. Share instances when students have been called names. How did it make them feel? How have they handled name-calling? Did others help to resolve the situation? In what ways? What are some responses that can help the target of the bullying diffuse the situation? How can schools take a stand against bullying? Display examples of manuscripts with illuminated (embellished) lettering from books about Middle Ages as well as contemporary illustrations. In small groups, brainstorm words or sentences that convey messages against name-calling and actions to take in response. Each student picks one idea to illuminate for a class book.		
Crayola® Supplies	• Construction Paper™ Crayons • Gel Markers • Glue Sticks • Metallic FX Colored Pencils • Scissors		
Other Materials	• Construction paper • Hole punch • Ribbon		

Hannah Illumination
Artist unknown
Ink on paper
6" x 6"
Collection of Hannah Willett.

Illuminated Manuscript
Circa 15th Century
Handpainted, ink on vellum
Private Collection.

Process: Session 1 20-30 min.	**Create leaf** 1. Cut black construction paper somewhat smaller than the sheet on which it will be mounted. Leave space to punch holes on the left side. 2. Design borders around edges of black pages. Draw decorative patterns—in the style of illuminated manuscripts—using Construction Paper Crayons, Metallic Colored Pencils, and Gel Markers. All of the colors are striking on black paper! 3. Enlarge and illuminate the first letter of the name-calling alternative message. 4. Fill leaf with more messages in a unifying style. Create designs with lines, shapes, colors, and patterns.		
Process: Session 2 30-40 min.	**Create manuscript page** 5. Punch holes in left margin of mounting pages. Make sure all pages are punched alike. Glue leaf to hole-punched paper. Air-dry the glue. 6. As a group, choose a title for the book and agree on the order in which the pages will appear. 7. In small groups, design the front cover, back cover, border for contributing authors' page, and table of contents. 8. Each student signs the authors' page.		
Process: Session 3 20-30 min.	**Assemble book** 9. Arrange pages in order. Add front matter and covers. 10. Thread ribbon through holes to bind book.		
Assessment	• Identify appropriate illumination and lettering styles. • Observe use of manuscript's ideas within classroom situations. • Ask students to reflect on this lesson and write a DREAM statement to summarize the most important things they learned.		
Extensions	With students, role-play common name-calling, bullying, and other hurtful situations. Agree on appropriate responses. Ask students to figure out what this saying means and whether they agree with it: "Sticks and stones can break my bones, but names can never hurt me." Together write sayings that are more suitable. Students with some types of disabilities may be more successful if they generate these materials on a computer.	Study some famous people who have been the target of name callers like Ruby Bridges. How did they handle it? Imagine what students would have done in those situations. Visit a printing plant and book-binder to learn more about the art of book production. Lead a school-wide anti-bullying effort. Engage student representatives, parents, teachers, and school administrators. Choose a mission and strategies that focus on supporting positive interactions within the school community.	Make manuscripts with a collage style instead of hand-drawn lettering. Debate whether the people who stand by and do nothing while name-calling or other bullying behavior happens are responsible to take action or not. Discuss past circumstances such as during the Civil Rights Movement as well as contemporary issues. Gifted students could prepare short skits to dramatize the hurtfulness of name-calling and possible solutions for reducing it. Perform before younger children and school families.

Illuminated Letters
Artist: Mary Wells
Watercolor on paper
4" x 4 1/2"
Collection of the artist.

The "Try Again" Marionette

Objectives
Students identify role models in fiction and real life who exemplify the character trait of perseverance.

Students use observation and knowledge of human proportions to create a marionette puppet to enact a story about perseverance.

Multiple Intelligences
- Bodily-kinesthetic
- Interpersonal
- Logical-mathematical
- **Naturalist**

What Does It Mean?
Proportions: relative size between two or more objects

Marionette: puppet manipulated from above by strings attached to its jointed limbs

Perseverance: steady persistence in a course of action, a purpose, a state in spite of dificulties, obstacles or discouragement

National Standards

Visual Arts Standard #2
Using knowledge of structures and functions

Visual Arts Standard #6
Making connections between the arts and other disciplines

Social Studies Standard #5
Individuals, Groups, and Institutions—experiences that provide for the study of interactions among individuals, groups, and institutions

Social Studies Standard #9
Global Connections- experiences that provide for the study of global connections and interdependence

Health Education Standard #2
Students will analyze the influence of family, peers, culture, media, technology, and other factors on health behaviors.

Background Information
Puppets have long been used in many cultures to tell stories that illustrate cultural values. The term *marionette* comes from the French meaning Little Mary, a reference to the stringed puppet that starred in the nativity story. Evidence of marionette puppets was found in Ancient Egypt. The early Catholic Church used puppets to tell Bible stories. The early English puppets of Punch and Judy evolved from the Italian Commedia dell'Arte puppet character of Pulchinella. North American Hopi and Zuni tribes create and use hand puppets to act out religious stories. TV shows since the 1950s such as *Kukla, Fran and Ollie; Howdy Doody; The Shari Lewis Show;* and *Sesame Street* use a wide variety of puppets to teach children positive behavior.

Resources

Easy to Make Puppets and How to Use Them
by Fran Rottman
Helpful tool with young children. Straightforward directions and classroom suggestions.

If Only I Could! by David Vision
Told from a young child's perspective, this is a simple story of perseverance gained through observation. Suitable for kindergarten and first grade.

Jim Henson's Designs and Doodles: A Muppet Sketchbook
by Alison Inches
An intimate, inspiring look at this imaginative artist's creative process through his sketches and more.

The Usborne Book of Puppets by Ken Haines
For 9- to 12-year-olds, this how-to-make puppets handbook has illustrated instructions and color photographs of finished products.

Vocabulary List
Use this list to explore new vocabulary, create idea webs, or brainstorm related subjects.

Body
Character
Marionette
Parts
Perform
Perseverance/
Persevere
Persistent
Play
Presentation
Proportion
Puppet
Show
Story
Storyteller

String
Succeed
Success
Trait

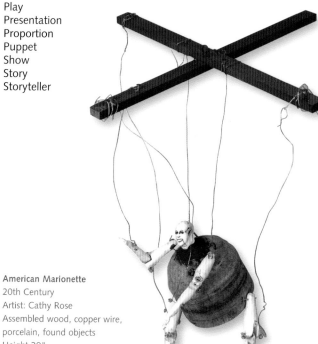

American Marionette
20th Century
Artist: Cathy Rose
Assembled wood, copper wire, porcelain, found objects
Height 20"
Orlando, Florida
Private Collection.

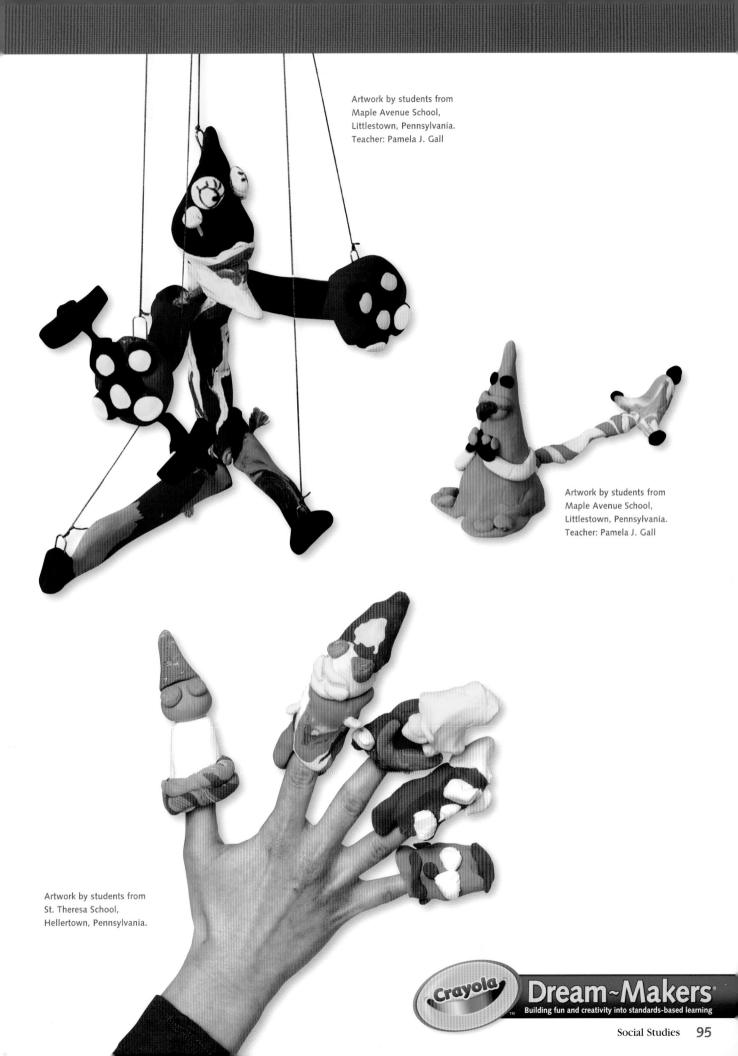

Artwork by students from
Maple Avenue School,
Littlestown, Pennsylvania.
Teacher: Pamela J. Gall

Artwork by students from
Maple Avenue School,
Littlestown, Pennsylvania.
Teacher: Pamela J. Gall

Artwork by students from
St. Theresa School,
Hellertown, Pennsylvania.

Crayola

Dream~Makers®
Building fun and creativity into standards-based learning

Social Studies   95

	K-2	3-4	5-6
Suggested Preparation and Discussion	Discuss the character trait of persistence. Ask students to share an example from their lives like learning how to ride a bike or joining a team. Compare the feelings one has when one stops trying to those when one keeps trying and succeeds.	Discuss the character trait of persistence. Share favorite books that support effort and persistence, such as *Aesop's Fables*, *The Wind in the Willows*, or *Shackleton's Valiant Voyage*. What are the pitfalls and rewards of persistent behavior?	Discuss the character trait of persistence. Examine popular culture for current examples of perseverance. Debate if students believe this trait is valued in our society today. Explore the notebooks of Leonardo da Vinci to learn more about his ideas about the proportions of the human body. Conduct simple measurement experiments to prove their validity.

As a class or in small groups, compose a puppet show about persistence drawn from real life experiences, literature, or pop culture. Design marionette characters to take part in the play.

Display pictures and examples of puppets from around the world and throughout history.

Crayola® Supplies
- Glitter Glue • Markers • Model Magic® • School Glue • Scissors

Other Materials
- Craft materials such as feathers and beads • Craft sticks • Chenille stems (optional)
- Modeling tools such as plastic dinner knives, craft sticks, and toothpicks
- Paper clips—large and small • Plastic drinking straws • String/cord

Set-up/Tips
- To protect and strengthen marionettes, coat them with a glaze of equal parts school glue and water.
- When stringing marionette, lay puppet on table to tie strings on to clips and handle.
- To keep strings untangled when not in use, gather action strings together with a piece of chenille stem.

Process: Session 1 20-30 min.

Form puppet body

1. Calculate proportions of puppet body parts. For example, a torso equals three heads. Mold a handful of Model Magic compound into the puppet torso and head unit.

2. Cover one end of a large paper clip with glue. Carefully insert it into the top of the puppet's head.

3. Squeeze top of puppet torso together until it is about 3/4-inch thick. Push a straw through, from one shoulder to other, making a hole for joining the arms.

4. Add texture with modeling tools. Using more Model Magic compound plus collage and craft materials, add facial features, clothing, and hair.

5. Follow the same procedure to make the bottom of torso. Push a straw from one hip to another for attaching the legs. Air-dry the parts at least 24 hours.

20th Century Czech Marionette
Artist unknown
Assembled wood, string, fabric, paint
24" x 8" x 6"
Private Collection.

	K-2	3-4	5-6

**Process:
Session 2
15-20 min.**

Form puppet's arms and legs

6. Form two separate arms with attached hands and two legs with attached feet. Insert small, glued paper clip ends into the tops of both hands and feet.

7. Poke holes in top of arms and legs with a straw. Add texture with modeling tools. Air-dry the puppet parts at least 24 hours.

**Process:
Session 3
10-15 min.**

8. Decorate the puppet with Glitter Glue. Air-dry.

**Process:
Session 4
20-30 min.**

String the puppet

9. With adult help, knot the end of cord and thread it through shoulder hole in one arm, through top torso hole, and finally through shoulder hole in other arm. Tie off cord to knot arms to torso.

10. Repeat Step 9 with hip area and legs.

11. Glue two craft sticks into an X. Air-dry the sticks.

12. While cross dries, tie cord to each paper clip. Cut each piece long enough to reach up to the control cross.

13. With adult assistance, tie head string to intersecting X. Wrap string around both sticks to reinforce it.

14. Tie hand strings to left and right ends of one stick and feet strings to other stick. Secure all knots with dots of glue. Air-dry glue before using marionettes in a class puppet show for which students design the stage sets.

Assessment

- Students can explain the character trait of perseverance and cite two examples of persistent behaviors.
- Students follow step-by-step directions to complete puppet construction.
- Ask students to reflect on this lesson and write a DREAM statement to summarize the most important things they learned.

Extensions

Physically challenged and younger students could form a Model Magic compound finger puppet. Press shape over finger. Add features and embellishments. Air-dry for 24 hours.

Collect sayings, slogans, and mottos about persistence. Learn more in children's home languages and from other cultures.

Plan a class trip to attend performances or visit online sites to see other types of puppet shows. Learn about the range of the art form including Vietnamese Water Puppets, Indonesian Shadow Puppets, Japanese Bunraku Puppets, and Taiwanese Glove Puppets.

Ask students to take persistence pledges, setting goals to persist at something until they succeed. Share successes at the end of the year in a perseverence notebook.

Write more episodes of puppet show for other character-building traits such as honesty and integrity. Adapt all plays to make into one film for distribution to other classes.

Gifted students may be interested in continuing exploration into the origins of measurement and its relationship to the human body. Study drawing techniques using these principles.

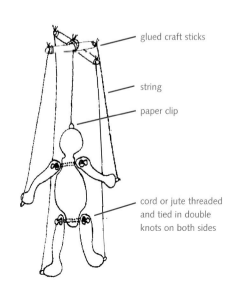

glued craft sticks

string

paper clip

cord or jute threaded and tied in double knots on both sides

No Matter How You Look at It!

Objectives

Students develop knowledge about the value of individual characteristics as they compare similarities and discover differences in living things.

Students design symmetrical butterflies to graphically depict their understanding about what is basic to all butterflies and what characteristics vary.

Multiple Intelligences

Interpersonal

Naturalist

What Does It Mean?

Batik effect: a technique of hand-dyeing paper by using a wax as a dye repellent to cover parts of a design. One covers a crumbled wax design on paper with a color or colors so the color adheres to the paper areas not covered with wax

Graphically depict: showing a clear and effective picture with bold strong emphasis

Symmetrical: the same on both sides of a center fold/axis

National Standards

Visual Arts Standard #6 Making connections between arts and other disciplines	Social Studies Standard #1 Culture—experiences that provide for the study of culture and cultural diversity. Social Studies Standard #8 Science, Technology, and Society—experiences that provide for the study of relationships among science, technology, and society. Health Education Standard #8 Students will demonstrate the ability to advocate for personal, family, and community health.

Background Information

Around the world, butterflies are different yet similar. For example, a variety of butterflies known as Male Birdwings live on Solomon Island of Papua New Guinea, and on Talaud Island of Indonesia. Although they come from different locations, they have similar wings, tails, bodies, and antennae. Upon closer examination one notices subtle differences in coloration, iridescence, lengths of tail spans, and hairiness of their bodies.

Resources

All the Colors of the Earth by Sheila Hamanaka
Rich oil paintings explore the diversity of the world's ethnic heritages. For students in grades 1 to 4.

Through My Eyes by Ruby Bridges
Powerful autobiography of a courageous 6-year-old. Brings the Civil Rights Movement to life for 8- to 12-year-olds.

We're Different, We're the Same by Bobbi Kates
For kindergartners and first graders. Celebrates human differences and similarities with colorful illustrations and an easy-to-read rhythm.

Vocabulary List

Use this list to explore new vocabulary, create idea webs, or brainstorm related subjects.

Butterfly
Cultural
Differences
Different
Diversity
Ethnic
Form
Gender
Global
Habit
Habitat
Heritage
Multicultural

Nationality
Open-minded
Patterns
Race
Religion
Same
Shape
Similarities
Symmetry
World

Artwork by students from
St. John Neuman School,
Palmerton, Pennsylvania.
Teacher: Paula Zelienka

Artwork by students from
Governor Wolf Elementary School,
Bethlehem, Pennsylvania.
Teacher: Patricia Check

Crayola Dream~Makers®
Building fun and creativity into standards-based learning

No Matter How You Look at It!

	K-2	3-4	5-6
Suggested Preparation and Discussion	Discuss what the world would be like if everyone looked the same. What if people all lived in similar houses? Differences make people noteworthy and yet there are things that we all share as human beings. For homework, ask students to carefully observe themselves and someone in their families. Note similarities and differences. With students, identify the body parts of a butterfly. Observe their unique colors, forms, and relative sizes. Investigate their habits and habitats. Compare and contrast what makes each butterfly distinctive.		Brainstorm a discussion about which students prefer—to be unique or the same as others? Lead students to understand that people are both different and same—and therein lies strength. Observe the unique shapes, colors, sizes, and forms of butterflies. Investigate their habits and habitats. Research the similarities and differences among various species of butterflies.
	Visit a butterfly garden to more fully appreciate the diversity of these magnificent creatures. Display pictures of butterflies from books and nature magazines.		
Crayola® Supplies	• Color Explosion™ White	• Crayons • Watercolor Paint	• Color Explosion Black
	• School Glue • Scissors		
Other Materials	• Clear adhesive tape	• Paper towels • Recycled newspaper • Water containers • White paper	• Clear adhesive tape
	• Tree branch		
Set-up/Tips		• Cover art surface with recycled newspaper.	• Work on a dry surface with dry hands.

Lepidoptera

BOLIVIA

Species –
Dismorphia nemesis

INDIA

Species –
Colias croceus v. edusina

BRAZIL

Species –
Automolis chrysomelas

INDIA

Species –
Anaphosis mesentian

BRAZIL

Species –
Phaloe cruenta

FORMOSA

Species –
Leche dura neoclides

MEXICO

Species –
Aeria eurimedia pacifico

BRAZIL

Species –
Phaloe cruenta

	K-2	3-4	5-6
Process: Session 1 10-15 min.	**Create butterfly** 1. Cut white Color Explosion Paper in half. Outline the shape of a butterfly with the Color Explosion Marker. Make sure the butterfly is big enough to fill the paper.	**Create butterfly** 1. Outline a large, detailed butterfly with a white crayon on drawing paper. Make the wings symmetrical.	**Create butterflies** 1. Cut black Color Explosion Paper in half. Outline a large, symmetrical butterfly with the Color Explosion Marker.

Process: Session 2 15-20 min.

Color butterfly

2. Look at the parts of a butterfly: the slender body, knobbed antennae, and four broad, usually brightly colored wings.

	K-2	3-4	5-6
	3. Color in the lines and shapes of wings and body. Add details with the black drawing marker.	3. Color in the lines and shapes of the butterfly with heavy layers of crayon, overlaying colors. 4. Crumple paper to make cracks. Dip in water. Squeeze out water. Flatten paper. 5. Brush paper with dark water-color paint. Blot page so dark paint remains in cracks for batik effect. Air-dry the butterflies.	3. Color in the lines and shapes of the wings and body.

Process: Session 3 10-15 min.

Display butterflies

Cut out butterflies. Tape them to a tree branch for display.

Assessment

- Students followed directions to create a symmetrical butterfly with all basic parts.
- Students can point out the similar physical aspects of their butterflies as well as identify their variety of colors, shapes, and patterns.
- Ask students to reflect on this lesson and write a DREAM statement to summarize the most important things they learned.

Extensions			
	Collect and learn songs about human diversity. Give a concert to promote cultural understanding. Children with some types of disabilities may find it helpful to look at a butterfly picture, or even trace it, as they draw and color. Do a similar lesson using children's pets, local indigenous animals, or some other topic in which children can readily observe diversity.	Create a butterfly swag by hanging the creations on ribbon. Display it in a large public area along with student statements about why they value diversity. Ask each student to bring one potato to class. After close observation, students write a description and sketch their potatoes. Students then match the potatoes to each other's descriptions.	Prepare a display of life-size, local butterflies, sculpted in Crayola Model Magic® compound. Gifted students could research to understand that in nature, although species are linked, it is their diversity that makes adaptability possible. Embark on a more in-depth study of Darwin's theories of species diversity.

Artwork by students from
St. John Neuman School,
Palmerton, Pennsylvania.
Teacher: Paula Zelienka

Crayola **Dream~Makers**®
Building fun and creativity into standards-based learning

The lessons in this guide suggest types of art materials. This chart outlines the specific characteristics of different Crayola art materials. Use it to choose which variation best meets your needs and those of your students.

CRAYONS/OIL PASTELS	CHARACTERISTICS
Regular Crayons (3-5/8" x 5/16")	• Brilliant colors; smooth, even color lay down.
Large Size Crayons (4" x 7/16")	• Brilliant colors; smooth, even color lay down. • Larger size for younger child palm grip.
Triangular Crayons	• Brilliant colors; smooth, even color lay down. • Triangular shape helps guide correct pincer grip. • Anti-roll.
Washable Crayons	• Brilliant colors; smooth, even color lay down. • Available in regular, large, and triangular sizes. • Superior washability from walls, tables, and most surfaces.
Construction Paper™ Crayons	• Brilliant colors; smooth, even color lay down. • Color shows on dark paper, brown craft paper, and similar surfaces.
Fabric Crayons	• Permanent when drawing is heat transferred to synthetic fabric.
Twistables® Crayons	• Brilliant colors; smooth, even color lay down. • Durable plastic barrel. • No sharpening with easy twist-up action.
Twistables Erasable Crayons	• Complete erasability of marks. • Brilliant colors; smooth, even color lay down. • Durable plastic barrel. • No sharpening with easy twist-up action. • Eraser on each crayon.
Twistables Slick Stix™ Crayons	• Super-smooth color glides on paper. • Water soluble upon application. • Dries quickly with no smearing. • Durable plastic barrel. • Great for older student crayon techniques. • Appropriate for students with special needs due to ease of color lay down.
Oil Pastels	• Opaque colors blend easily. • Good color lay down. • Hexagonal shape prevents rolling.
Portfolio® Series Oil Pastels	• Opaque colors blend and layer well, with velvety lay down. • Unique water solubility allows watercolor washes.

MARKERS	CHARACTERISTICS
Regular Markers	• Bright, brilliant, transparent colors. • Conical tip draws thick and thin lines. • Fine tip draws thin lines and detail.
Washable Markers	• Washability you can trust™–superior washability from hands and most clothing. • Bright, brilliant, transparent colors. • Conical tip draws thick and thin lines. • Fine tip draws thin lines and detail. • Wedge tip provides ease in broad strokes and vertical applications.
Gel Markers	• Bright, opaque colors that deliver bold marks on black and dark papers. • World's most washable marker with superior washability from hands and most clothing. • Writes on glass, foil, glossy, and other non-porous surfaces. • Conical tip draws thick and thin lines.
Overwriters® Markers	• Bright "overcolors" magically color over darker "undercolors" for exciting and dramatic effects.
Color Changeables™ Markers	• Students have fun seeing colors magically "pop out" over each other for new creative expression possibilities. • Increased color variety as "wand" changes 7 colors to 7 new colors.
Twistables Markers	• No lost caps! • Bright, brilliant, transparent colors.
Fabric Markers	• Permanent bright color on cotton or cotton blends when heat set. • Bullet tip for medium and fine detail.
Dry-Erase Markers	• Low odor, bold color that can be viewed from a distance. • Chisel and bullet tips.

COLORED PENCILS	CHARACTERISTICS
Colored Pencils	• Bright, vivid colors with opaque lay down. • Good blending. • Thick 3 mm lead; made from reforested wood.
Watercolor Colored Pencils	• Water soluble for watercolor and drawing effects. • Bright, vivid colors with opaque lay down. • Good blending. • Thick 3 mm lead; made from reforested wood.
Erasable Colored Pencils	• Complete erasability of pencil marks. • Bright colors with opaque lay down. • Good blending. • Eraser on each pencil. • Thick 3 mm lead; made from reforested wood.
Twistables Colored Pencils	• Bright colors; smooth, even color lay down. • Durable plastic barrel. • No sharpening with easy twist-up action.
Twistables Erasable Colored Pencils	• Complete erasability of pencil marks. • Bright colors; smooth, even color lay down. • Durable plastic barrel. • No sharpening with easy twist-up action. • Eraser on each pencil.
Write Start® Colored Pencils	• Thick 5.3 mm lead and large hexagonal barrel is great for young students. • Bright, vivid colors with opaque lay down. • Anti-roll. • Made from reforested wood.

MODELING COMPOUNDS	CHARACTERISTICS
Air-Dry Clay	• No firing, air-dry clay. • Good for high-detail projects. • Natural clay body to create solid, durable forms. • Suitable for all clay techniques. • White color suitable for all color/surface decoration. • Air-dries hard.
Model Magic®	• Soft, easy-to-manipulate compound. • Good for low-detail projects. • Good for young students and those who are developing manual dexterity. • Air-dries to consistency of a foam cup.
Modeling Clay	• Traditional oil-based clay. • Non-hardening and reusable.

PAINTS	CHARACTERISTICS
Premier™ Tempera	• Ultimate opacity and coverage. • Creamy consistency flows smoothly and will not crack or flake. • Intense, true hues for accurate color mixing.
Artista II® value-priced Tempera	• Fine-quality colors with good opacity. • Creamy consistency flows smoothly and will not crack or flake. • Good hue positions for excellent color mixtures. • Washable from skin and fabrics.
Washable Paint	• Washability you can trust™–superior washability from skin and fabrics. • Bright, clean colors for consistent color mixing. • Smooth-flowing formula will not crack or flake.
Acrylic Paint	• Pigment-rich colors are intense even when diluted; achieve accurate color mixes. • Thick, tube-like viscosity, for a variety of techniques from air-brushing to impasto. • Permanent, water resistant, and flexible when dry.
Washable Finger Paint	• Bright colors, thick consistency. • Washable from skin and fabrics.
Watercolors	• Bright, intense, transparent colors. • True hues for accurate color mixing. • Ideal for opaque and transparent techniques.
Washable Watercolors	• Washability you can trust–superior washability from skin and fabrics. • Bright, intense, transparent colors.